信仰

JESUS CULTURE

TOOLKIT:

JAPAN MISSIONS GUIDEBOOK

SPECIAL EDITION

Includes over **100 scriptures** regarding believing
and trusting God to help build your faith!

JAMES XAVIER

Dedicated to my wife Tracy who has loved me unconditionally for decades. She is my love and my ministry partner who has made life in Japan so much more enjoyable for me and for our children because of her humor, dedication and service.

"The earth is the Lord's, and all its fullness,
The world <u>and those who dwell therein</u>."

Psalm 24:1 (NKJV)

Ordering Information/Quantity sales:
Special discounts are available on quantity purchases by corporations, associations, and others. For details, contact the author at the email address above.

Printed in the United States of America

TABLE OF CONTENTS

FOREWARD

When most people hear the word, *"missions," "missionary,"* or *"mission field,"* Japan is *probably not* what first comes to mind, if at all. This is not surprising since Japan is not a third world nation, where food, clean water and clothing are lacking. Japan also has fairly low unemployment and low crime rates.

As well, Japan is not known to be a short-term missions destination where a feeding program, well-digging or building project would be needed. There are relatively few churches in Japan, with many of these not having any ties to churches or groups in the USA or other western nation. Unless a church is pioneered or led by a foreign missionary, a connection to an outside organization is rare.

Another reason one might not first consider Japan for missions work is that Japan is extremely expensive. Tokyo surpasses Manhattan prices in terms of real-estate, food and general cost of living. Since Japan is an island nation, residents of Japan experience high prices daily, with gasoline as much as $7.00 per gallon. Quality fruits such as organically grown apples often cost as much as $4.00 each. This is not uncommon, and the general cost of living follows suit. Therefore, sending a missionary to Japan can not only be costly, but it requires lots of time, energy and commitment to make a significant impact.

Perhaps you are thinking, "What an introduction to Japan! Few churches, expensive, workers needed . . . Why on earth would I go to Japan!?"

Well, let me share with you the other side of the coin: *Japan needs Jesus as much as anyone else on the planet.* Their culture has been trapped in centuries of old religion and customs, often making the move to Christianity difficult due to peer and family pressure. The Japanese are an incredible race of people, with so much to share and teach the world about honor, respect, patience and quality. As Christians, I believe the Japanese would be an unstoppable force for God! As Christians, their cultural assets would become *assets for God*, affecting not only the surface and things visceral, but the spiritual and the deepest parts of humanity; things eternal.

When I look at the Japanese people, I liken it to the description found in Matthew 9 when Jesus looked out at the masses:

> *"When He saw the crowds, He felt compassion for them, because they were <u>weary and worn out</u>, like sheep without a shepherd."*
> —Matthew 9:36, HCSB

The Japanese priority list starts with WORK. The Japanese believe very much in the rewards of working hard and resting little. But from this we can teach an important lesson, a great motivator in the spirit.

"For no one can lay any other foundation than what has been laid down. That foundation is Jesus Christ. If anyone builds on that foundation with gold, silver, costly stones, wood, hay, or straw, each one's work will become obvious, for the day will disclose it, because it will be revealed by fire; the fire will test the quality of each one's work." —1 Corinthians 3:11-15 HCSB

The Japanese work very hard, and are therefore often tired and weary, especially mothers of small children and *salarymen* (company employees) who have to work late into the night. A common sight in Japan is people sleeping on public transportation. I often see people asleep at restaurants, malls, bus stops and other places one might not expect to see such a thing. They are tired, both inside and out, and only Jesus can bring true rest through true peace.

Presently, Japan is about 1.5% Christian, but many believers expect and trust God to change that statistic very soon! So as of today, the Japanese as a nation are 99% eternally lost! 127 million people, with almost 126 million without Jesus Christ as their Savior. Comparatively speaking, very few Christian workers live in Japan to convey the message of God's love.

The Japanese basic model for all points in life can be summed up in the unofficial national motto of, *"Ganbatte,"* which means, *"do your best"* or *"persevere."* Of course we should try always to do our best, but even our best does not bring us closer to God or to salvation.

Often the inside of a person does not match the outside. I liken it to erecting a beautiful building upon which hangs a sign that reads, *"This building was designed for amazing purposes."* But the inside of the building is incomplete with exposed beams, dangerous areas, loose wiring, all kinds of damage, and smells from years of stagnancy.

Souls not purged through the cleansing blood of Jesus Christ are souls with amazing eternal potential, but are otherwise just lost souls walking around without hope, purpose and direction. Their outside may reflect hard work, national pride, attention to detail and financial security, but the inside may be dark, damp and damaged. And without Jesus as our Savior, we are all incomplete.

What is the value of a soul? Obviously it is worth more than a gallon of gasoline, and more than an overly-priced apple. The value of a soul is *priceless*, so I wrote this book to encourage you to see that we can believe God for the impossible. We can literally be blessed beyond measure in giving our own lives away through serving, sharing, denying ourselves so that others may live a fuller life in Christ. I pray that as you read this, whether you are interested in serving in Japan or elsewhere, that your faith is edified, that your conscience is made aware and that your heart increases in passion for the work of the ministry of international missions. God bless you and thank you for reading!   --James Xavier

INTRODUCTION

How to Use This Book / Description

This book was written from personal experience and from the anecdotes of others. It contains scripture and key thoughts to motivate your spiritual life and pursuit in missions work, focusing on, but not limited to, missions work in Japan.

Keep a Bible handy as you read. This book is packed with scriptures that you will want to read for yourself. By using your Bible while reading, your faith will rise and you will be able to confirm all of what is written here by God's own Word.

Part One: Introduction

The first portion of this book was written with great hopes to inspire you, to help take the weight of the impossible seem altogether possible. Jesus said in Matthew 19:26, *"with men this is impossible, but with God all things are possible."* This and many other verses will serve as our ship of faith, riding over the crest of cultures, customs and traditions, plunging our oars of truth into seas of darkness. Jesus is our captain, providing the power, boldness, and passion through the Holy Spirit. God has given us all of the tools needed to bridge cultural barriers.

Part Two: The Reconciliation of Japan

The second portion is actually where this writing started, but it was composed long before the idea for this book you are now holding came together as a single work. Written before I had ever visited Japan, I was inspired to write a faith-based short story regarding the future of Japan under the lordship of Jesus Christ. I felt at the time it was important for me to challenge my own level of faith with something that *seemed impossible* so that I would not limit myself to what I felt God could do, but to look at what He really can do, according to His Word. I wanted to see in my mind's eye those things which I felt I had understood in scripture, but needed to visualize it further. It is meant to encourage all who believe the Bible is true, and to give God glory and thanksgiving for His unending love for mankind.

Part Three: Japan Missions Guidebook

The third component of this book is the nuts and bolts of it all, the "Japan Missions Guidebook." It was written from a training perspective for those desiring to minister in Japan. In it, I share some cultural, historical and practical information to help those interested in or currently serving the Japanese people. As you draw closer to the Japanese people and understand this amazing culture and mind set even more, God will surely open your eyes to new and exciting ways to reach out.

Part Four: Relocating & Getting Settled

The fourth part contains more information which will be helpful to starting the process of moving abroad.

Part Five: Final Thoughts

This section details final thoughts on various things to consider such as eduction for your children, keeping spiritually fit while serving overseas, and what life might be like for you in Japan.

I pray that God would use this book to help you in your missions journey, whether it be in Japan or some other wonderful country around the world. Maybe even your own country or a part of your city.

TESTIMONY: HOW GOD BROUGHT US TO JAPAN

This is the expanded testimony of how we first sensed God's presence in our lives regarding Japan, and the events which followed from 2003 to the present.

In 2003, my wife Tracy and I began having dreams at night. They were vivid and between the two of us, very similar. Tracy dreamt of rescuing Japanese by carrying them on our backs, delivering them from a dangerous disaster such as a fire. She also dreamt of nurturing adults like babies, feeding them milk and ushering them to safety. I dreamt of standing on multiple Japanese bridges, with various pieces of imagery bringing our dreams together. One night in fact, we had the same dream. God was beginning to open our eyes to His calling. But we didn't know it. We both journaled these dreams and kept our spiritual ears open.

It wasn't until 2005 where I sensed an increase of passion for the Japanese. This came by way of Him speaking very deeply one word into my spirit: *"Japan."* I heard it while in prayer, kneeling alongside my bed one afternoon. It was a shaking of my innermost being, and I knew it was not my own thoughts but the Lord speaking. After this, immediately my personal passion for understanding the Japanese increased daily, and I hungered to know more about life in Japan, the culture, religion, Christianity. Our burden for the souls of the Japanese was increasing.

It was around this time that God gave us a divine appointment to meet the missionaries with whom, at the time of the writing of this book, we are now working -- Nils and Andrea Olson. It began while meeting with Retta, one of our prayer workers at church, the Holy Spirit moved me to ask her if she knew anyone in Japan. She paused and said flatly, "no, I don't." But then in a flash it came to her and she remembered receiving a booklet from Nils that he had written many years earlier and was distributing in the US while on furlough. Retta still had a copy. She dashed home, found the copy and gave it to me. Written in pre-Internet era, the only information I had was the church's name and address. I Googled, *"Nils Olson Munakata Bethel Christian Center."* . . . Found it. The link took me to an all-Japanese web page with a very small space to send a comment from the site. Not knowing if this was actually the right place or not, I took a chance and sent a long message about our dreams, passions and thoughts on Japan up until that time. We wondered if we were called to Japan or what this might mean. We wondered if anyone would ever reply.

The next day, I came into work to find my desk voice mail light flashing, indicating I had received a message. It was from Pastor Nils. The message went something like this: "Hi, this is Nils Olson, you had sent a message through our web site and we would absolutely *love* to speak with you and your wife. We happen to be in Federal Way right now (a neighboring city), so let's get together for lunch and talk." Federal Way? All the way from Japan and they were just moments away! God, what could you be doing? Our minds started to reel with thoughts of where things could go from here, but yet we did not try to force God's hand or convince ourselves of anything that God did not personally speak to our own hearts.

Jim, Tracy, Retta, Andrea and Nils, first meeting

On August 8, 2006, Tracy, I and our friend Retta, met with Pastor Nils and Andrea at Marie Callender's retaurant in Federal Way. We talked for hours sharing and getting to know each other.

The Olsons suggested we take a trip to Japan, so in April, 2007 we took our first trip to Japan to put our feet on the ground and pray. We learned a lot and shared our experience with our friends and family at River of Life, our home church in Kent, WA.

Some time later on, Tracy and I opened our home to a Japan missions fellowship group, praying for Japan and introducing the group to facts about Japan. We did everything we could to be open to God, to lead us and also to encourage us to pray for Japan and for the Japanese. But another step was needed. We took another trip to Japan in 2010, this time intensely seeking the Lord for an answer on what to do.

It was in July, 2010 on our last night visiting the Olsons in Japan when the Lord spoke to us about making a move. Tracy and I were lying in bed talking when the Spirit of the Lord moved once again to confirm the timing. He gave us a very clear word that it was time to move, now. We landed in the US, urgent to share with our pastors God's desire for us to move to Japan. It was a difficult separation as Tracy and I both had been on staff with our church for several years prior, so our working and friendship relationship with our pastors and staff was intimate.

But with the help and support of our home church, the agreement of our church board, and the financial support, love and prayers of so many, we were launched into full time missions work.

Much prayer followed, and plans were put in place. We sold or gave away most of our personal belongings and raised money. We received our passports, applied for our visas and away we went, arriving in Japan on January 18, 2011.

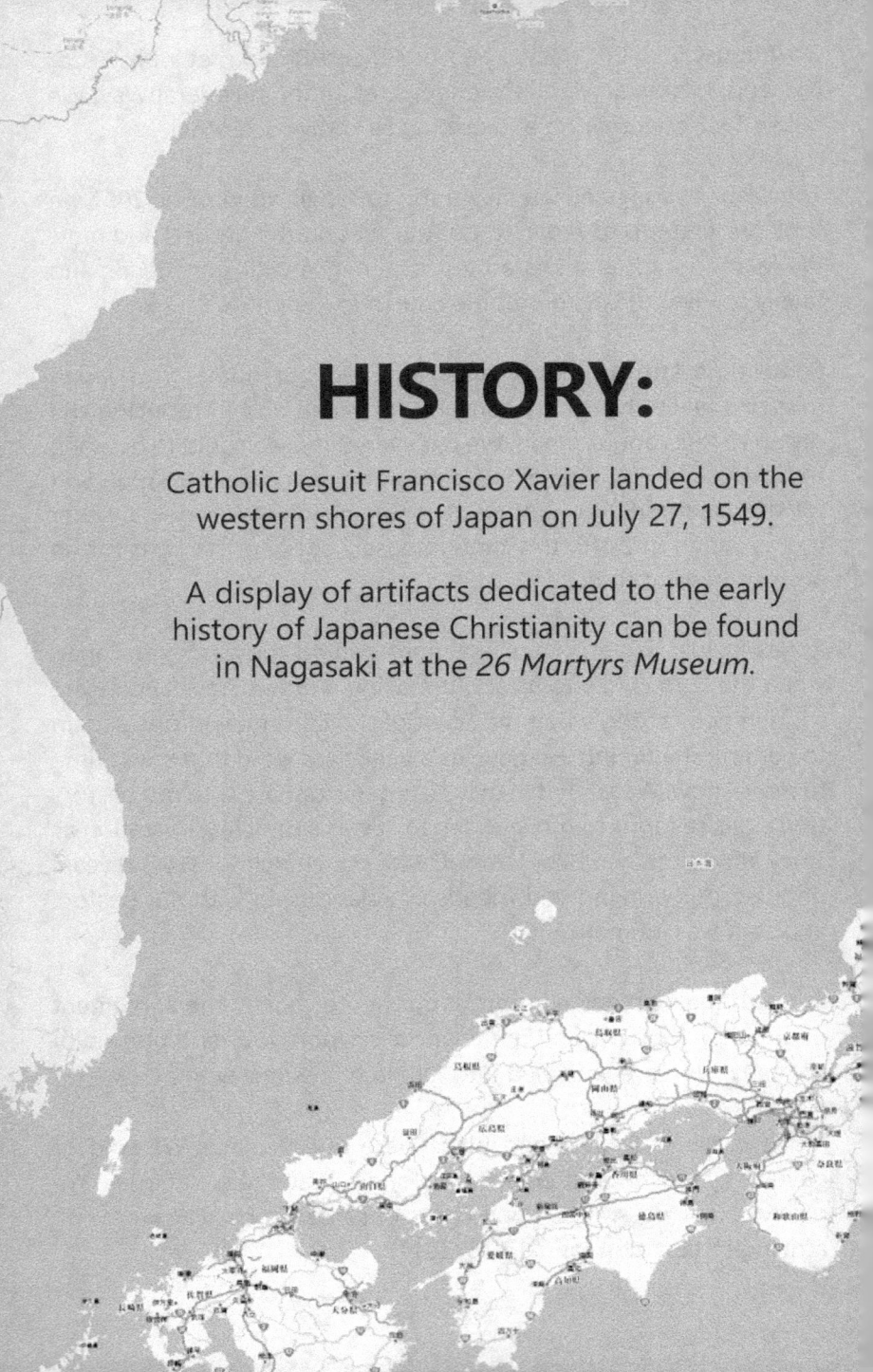

HISTORY:

Catholic Jesuit Francisco Xavier landed on the western shores of Japan on July 27, 1549.

A display of artifacts dedicated to the early history of Japanese Christianity can be found in Nagasaki at the *26 Martyrs Museum*.

日本
NI HON
(JAPAN)

PART ONE:
JESUS CULTURE TOOLKIT

Communication barriers stink.

I have been climbing over one for years as I learn Japanese, sometimes wondering if I am saying what I mean or worse yet, being misunderstood completely. Even for fluent speakers, this is sometimes a problem in communicating just the right word, or right nuance in what one is intending to convey. Even in my native language of English, there are times when I am misunderstood!

Cultural barriers can be even more challenging because they go beyond the verbal realm and into the traditional and often spiritual realms of people's lives. Traditions are strong, and many are good. Traditions can center around family, seasons, music or just about anything. But the most powerful and meaningful are spiritual traditions and customs. This is because the spiritual surpasses logic, moving us to a place of faith in the *unseen*. This applies, mind you, not only to Christians. Let me explain.

Children are often taught spiritual principles of *faith* which are never questioned because they are usually not examined in that light. Many kids around the world are taught to believe in various entities, spirits, stories, legends, and so on. So these things then become <u>spiritually familiar</u> and <u>culturally familiar</u> because they are a natural part of our lives from a young age. As these children grow up and teach their children, a new cultural bond is birthed and the cycle continues for generations. In a very homogeneous society such as Japan, this cyclical reinforcement is in part what has built the barriers and bondage we see today.

Japan is an island nation, full of rich history and culture. It is also a land of controversy, and contradiction. For example, Japan is world-famous for its technology exports and cars, but also for its high suicide rate and booming pornography industry. It offers top-notch customer service, but if you ask, for example, for extra pickles on your burger at the local Moss Burger® restaurant, the answer is invariably, "Sorry, we can't do that." Even though they have pickles, they won't add them because the menu has been decided. So in this there is a compromise: you *will* receive good service, *but* only as dictated by the *company policies*, not the customer's actual desires. Everything has been predetermined and locked down. So what should be an easy fix (extra pickles) in the customer's mind turns into a matter of settled *policy*, translating across the counter as seemingly apologetic, but in the end, unwaivering. "Shigatta ga nai, (仕方がない)" means in Japanese, "It cannot be helped/changed."

A friend once told me that Japanese are the "most flexible Christians" because they are able to believe in other religions and in Jesus simultaneously. The Bible says we cannot serve two masters (Matt 6:24). So even though the statement was a nice sentiment, it is scripturally in error and should not be construed as something constructive, but quite the opposite when it comes to faith in God.

The culture of Japan is unique in its own details, and like all nations, its culture is what sets it apart. Japan's foundations, traditions and rules have made Japan what it is today; a nation of many etiquette do's and don'ts; a largely unified body steeped in obligation and form. As such, not following certain patterns of expected behavior often results in shame and the appearance of selfishness when not conformed to the overall group welfare.

It is because of ancient, but yet-maintained traditions and customs that missionaries tend to find harvesting the Japanese mission field a difficult task. And although many will clearly agree that scripture is true and that salvation is for all, the same will also agree that the culture of Japan is intensely strong and difficult to "bridge" or better yet, override. I am writing to you today, dear missions-minded worker, to remind all of us that *Jesus Culture* is indeed stronger than *any* national culture, Japan or otherwise; that the

"*These are challenges which are meant to be confronted with the Word of God and the Living Truth of that Word.*"

Spirit of God is stronger than *any* other spirit, idol or false God —no matter how big, how old or how revered; and that every culture is bridgeable by love, peace, and the power that comes only from above. A true disciple of Jesus is known by their fruit, so this is our goal: to make disciples <u>fully and completely</u>. Disciples which reproduce. If we make lukewarm disciples, they will fall back into the likewise lukewarm pool of familiarity from which they were set free. This means, then, that we ourselves must be spiritually ablaze for God for this chain reaction to occur in others (Rev. 3:16).

Bridging a cultural barrier is difficult, but not impossible. It comes with challenges, but these are challenges which are meant to be confronted with the Word of God and the Living Truth of that Word. This is our focus in moving forward in this book.

"A psalm of David. The earth is the LORD's, and everything in it. The world and all its people belong to him." (Psalm 24:1)

For God SO LOVED the WORLD that He gave His only Son to die for us. He loves every nation on earth, and He understands all religions, cultures, languages and every detail therein. Nothing is a surprise to God and nothing is too great for His mighty hand. Please remember how big God is compared to all else, and what will move these seemingly impossible mountains is <u>faith to believe</u> in what He can and will do. Don't focus on the barrier—focus on seeing the other side in faith. Hebrews 11:1 tells us that faith is the *"substance of things hoped for, the EVIDENCE of things NOT SEEN."*

In a court of law, evidence is what is used to prove a case. So how can we have evidence of things not seen? Aha! Such is faith! It is the opposite of what we *do* see, for we can easily believe in the existence of things which are visible. But how about the invisible which has not yet come to pass? **This is the panoramic lens of faith.** It sees what the eyes do not see, and believes what the mind cannot fathom. It changes life in a realm beyond finite reason and agrees not with our soulish minds but with Holy Scripture. Faith is a miracle from God and it is to be revered and respected as any other miracle we have ever known. It is a direct offering from the heavenlies, given to us to use for life-changing purposes. Faith is amazing. I believe if more Christians could get ahold of true faith, this planet would change more rapidly than we ever realized possible. —Let's do it!

In terms of sharing Jesus with others, culture in and of itself is not the problem. God was there when all forms of culture began, and he understands the evolution of all cultures. And for all that God intends for good, often men pervert and distort for their own purposes. This has been the case since the Garden of Eden where disobedience, blame and sin entered our lives. The darkened hearts of men is the true problem (Ephesians 4:18). It is the thoughts and hearts of men that create, foster and preserve culture. But slithering through unguarded crevices of men's hearts lurks a form of godlessness known as the *spirit of antichrist*. This spirit gains access to culture by way of men's hearts which are devoid of God. 1 John 4:3 explains the basis of this evil spirit:

"And every spirit that confesseth not that Jesus Christ is come in the flesh is not of God: and this is that spirit of antichrist, whereof ye have heard that it should come; and <u>even now already is it in the world</u>."

This spirit is what *strips culture* of any ties to Jesus Christ. It tries desperately to purge God and godliness from the origins of original form, which is that which God created for His own pleasure. This antichrist spirit is indeed powerful and grows more powerful as the end of time draws near. This means that our challenge to combat the powers of darkness also grows more intense. Scripture does not paint a very lovely picture from here on out. We have a war on our hands. So to fight a difficult battle, we need big guns in our arsenal—and we have them!

I wish I could express the joy I feel in writing this right now. God is with you in your journey, and with these weapons of war in your heart and in your hands, you are an incredible force in Him! These are the three big "guns" we will keep with us at all times. These weapons of spiritual warfare are fully loaded and powerful beyond measure:

> *"This combination is like a truckload of dynamite. . . . Would you like to crash into that? "*

1) **Jesus Christ as our Savior**, our firm Foundation on which to stand (John 12:44, John 14:1, Acts 2:21, Acts 4:12, Romans 10:9-10).

2) **A solid understanding of the Word of God.**
(Proverbs 4:7, 1 Corinthians 4:15, 2 Timothy 2:15, Proverbs 2:3-6).

3) **Faith to believe** in the Truth found in the Word of God (Hebrews 11:1, Romans 1:17, Mark 11:23, John 11:40, Matthew 21:22, Luke 17:6, Mark 10:27, Philippians 4:13).

There are other weapons of spiritual warfare, all important and all are available to us at any time. Love, prayer, and to walk according to the Spirit in all ways. This combination is like a truckload of dynamite. Would you like to crash into that? You would be blown to smithereens! This is what we want the spirit of antichrist to do when it confronts us, to be blown to bits because of *the power we possess* in The Holy Spirit, not of ourselves. We will cause a spiritual counterculture explosion in the heavenlies which confounds and confuses the enemy of our souls. How? By acting in faith using the precious name of Jesus Christ. This evokes unlimited, supernatural power.

CULTURE CLASH

As early on as the great exodus in Exodus 32, we see a God upset with His own people, calling them "stiff necked." And the same term is heard at the stoning of Stephen during his speech before the Sanhedrin (Acts 7:51). The religious rulers of Jesus' day—the Scribes, Pharisees and Sadducees, were known to be the most religious, yet the least aware of who Jesus was. Their eyes were blinded to the truth. Why? Because of their *religious culture* which was commingled with the spirit of antichrist. This is shown in the fact that there were Jews then who *did* believe in Jesus, and there are yet Jews today who *still* believe. Yet not all do because of tradition and custom which does not include Jesus, the author of all Truth. Paradoxical indeed, but this historic clash of culture and religion was only the beginning of some very interesting times in history which lay ahead.

Jesus faced cultural and spiritual barriers which ended in His death. However the counter-cultural element that seemed as though it had won the battle against the Son of God was working in accordance with the will of God all along. Jesus then conquered the grave and ascended on high to reign forevermore. It was only after this that the Holy Spirit was given to us to empower us for *even greater cultural spiritual battles* such as those we face today in Japan and elsewhere.

China is home to the largest worldwide Christian church in terms of numbers of believers, ranging from 18 million (government calculation) to 150 million (as reported by Xiaowen Ye, head of the Communist Party's State Administration of Religious Affairs).

Regardless of the actual number, Christianity as a faith goes against the established Communist government philosophies. This is a direct parallel to the spirit of antichrist, which does not want Christians or anyone else to conform to the ways of God, suppressing with a cultural choke hold.

Yet the believers in China are hungry for God. So hungry that they risk their lives to simply taste salvation and to partake of the Truth of His Word. I don't know about you, but that is a humbling thought to me and causes me to wish never to take the Word of God and my access to it for granted!

The Chinese church numbers grow exponentially each year. How? Even with a culture which makes Christianity very difficult with harsh persecution, it is flourishing because of their pure desire for God, matched with His will to meet them right where they are. This is the ultimate illustration of the difference between religion and relationship. These are "hot" disciples, sold out to the end.

THE RISE OF JESUS CULTURE

Let's now traverse across the globe and take a look at the United States. An extensive new survey by the Pew Forum on Religion & Public Life details statistics on religion in America and explores the shifts taking place in the U.S. religious landscape. Based on interviews with more than 35,000 Americans ages 18 and older, the U.S. Religious Landscape 2013 Survey finds that religious affiliation in the U.S. is both very diverse and extremely *fluid*.

According to Pew Research, the United States religious landscape breaks down into some interesting bits and pieces. 78% claim to be Christian, 51.3% Protestant. From that, 26.3% are Evangelical. All other non-Christian religions in the U.S. make up only 4.7% and only 1.6% profess to be atheist. Looking at the top-line figure versus the atheist, that's **a 76.4 point lead.** Yet we do not seem to be leading spiritually by most accounts. The non-Christian/atheist agenda is leading the way in politics, social issues and even dominating religion for the most part.

This is not to say that great things are not being done to advance the Kingdom of God. Many wonderful things happen every day with people accepting Christ as their Savior while acts of love and kindness abound. However, the antichrist spirit is busily at work to attack any remnant of truth found anywhere. Remember, this spirit of antichrist is out to remove the truth anywhere it can. And if it can disguise itself as the truth in order to keep people from seeing the *real* truth, it will

" . . . we in turn must move swiftly to introduce world culture to Jesus culture and watch the fireworks begin. "

because people are hungry for something more than what they have now.

These statistics are interesting to note, but let me splash some cold water on our faces to remind us once again that we do not walk according to these facts and figures (the things that we see). These figures are based on actual surveys taken. However to win the war, we walk by faith in *that evidence which we do not see*. It is powerful because as large as your faith is, God will do even more (Ephesians 3:20), and that is truth from God's Word that cannot be shaken.

So why did I include this seemingly sad survey? Only to show you that the world is moving very quickly and we in turn must move swiftly to introduce world culture to *Jesus culture* and watch the fireworks begin. I would like to share a personal testimony with you before concluding the first part of this book.

TESTIMONY: MARDI GRAS

My wife Tracy and I served as missionaries to America in 1998 with Heart-Fire Ministries when we took a trip to Mardi Gras in New Orleans. I had not really understood what Mardi Gras was—until we arrived. We were told that it was basically a big party, and that people did some ludicrous things in public at this giant bash that lasted sometimes two weeks or longer. The main portions of the event leading up to Mardi Gras Day itself, or "Fat Tuesday," lasts three days and increases each day with intensity in drinking, hostility and sexual activity. It hosts parades, live music, loads of alcohol, and just about every form of weirdness that could be seen. More than four million people converge in Louisiana for this annual celebration in costumes and garb of all kinds.

After three hours or prayer and worship each day, Tracy and I hit the streets of this powerful (and very spiritually dark) event as fairly new Christians. We were not sure how our new walk with Christ would fare in this spiritually competitive climate. We were not the only Christians there. Many groups came to "witness" to people, but with giant signs that said things like "God Hates Gays" and "Repent or Go to Hell." We were disturbed by our Christian brothers and sisters using heavy-handed religion to condemn those we were trying to help. We took a very simple approach: love people and talk with them through this love. The results were as we believed: amazing.

THE GOTH TEENS
We spoke with a handful of teens hanging out under a stairwell, some dressed like vampires, some appeared homeless. They asked us if we were Christians "like those guys"—the ones with the condemning signs. We told them we were not with those people, but we were in fact Christians, but with a different message. We told them that they are loved by God, that they are very special; that He cared about them. We gave them some tracts and literature but before we left, one of the kids told us that they really appreciated

us and that they were glad we talked to them. A seed was planted.

THE HOMOSEXUAL MAN

I had a one-on-one conversation with a homosexual man. It started off the same way with him asking if I was out to "convert him." I asked him if we could sit down for just 5 minutes. He hesitated, but then shifted to flattery, telling me I was handsome. I could feel the spirit of antichrist reaching out to avert my mission to share the Truth of Jesus with this man. By the Spirit of God, I was led to share with him in a word of knowledge that I understood his past and knew he was desperate for a father. I told him that there is a Father who loves Him and cares for him. So much that He gave Jesus to cover his sins and to free him from a life of difficulty and strife. His eyes were like glass, and his heart warmed. He ended the conversation telling me it was too difficult to stop being gay, and that he didn't like his life but he was content to be in it. He left by saying I was the nicest person he had ever met. It was a nice thing for him to say, but it saddened me because I spent only 5 minutes with him and that was the most kindness he had seen in his 25 or so years of life. A kind word was spoken in due season.

THE SUICIDAL MAN

We witnessed a suicidal man about to jump from a bridge, dressed in a tuxedo to celebrate his last day on earth, turn his life around for Christ—and in the same day handed out tracts with us, telling people how *Jesus literally saved his life* that day. God loves everyone.

THE PSYCHIC

We witnessed a "veteran" psychic in Jackson Square give his life to Christ by way of the faith of a tiny little lady on our team named Jackie. Jackie pursued this man with great love and no fear. You could see that he hated her, until the love of Jesus melted his heart and he folded up his little fortune-telling card table and retired his life of spiritual deception. Love covers a multitude of sins.

THE DRINKERS

We witnessed two drunk young men, with whom we were sharing, literally sober up in front of our eyes, put down their giant Mardi-Gras-sized drinks on the ground, and walk away saying they could not drink alcohol in our presence. God's light scatters the darkness.

We sang and shouted praises from an open-air amphitheater facing the French Quarter, declaring the joy and goodness of God over the people partying, seeking the Lord to free them and open their eyes. And God did it. Not for us, but for Him. We enjoyed the benefit of seeing our faith come alive, but God was out to draw the people to himself. *He needed our help to bring that awareness to them*, so we did what we could and He did the rest.

Looking back, Mardi Gras paints an almost tangible spiritual picture. Unaccountable behavior, a hedonistic view of sex and a 100% pursuit of the flesh. Satanic influence was everywhere. Spiritual oppression filled the air. We were attacked physically, urinated on and called names as we walked down the streets. It was an experience we will never forget. But the most powerful things about which we boast are those things that **God did** in the midst of it all.

THE CULTURE OF ANTICHRIST

I shared this testimony because in the same way, the culture of Japan is strong as steel but *not unbridgeable*. But it does take time to understand this complex and winding road of the mind with traditions and customs binding tightly the thoughts of the people of Japan.

The satanic cloud of antichrist counterfeits The Holy Spirit, acting as a form of comfort without actually comforting. It counterfeits our Heavenly Father, offering a place of refuge without true protection. It counterfeits our Savior Jesus Christ by taking life instead of giving life. It deceives, takes and destroys while compounding guilt, shame and dead-end religion—all the while convincing people into thinking this is a good thing. It takes everything and gives nothing in return. *This is antichrist.*

WAGING WAR ON THE ENEMY OF OUR SOULS

The Japanese are often imprisoned by the culture of the past, worshipping objects, ancestors and false gods. They deserve to be free, because they too were bought for a price on the cross. With wisdom from above, and with our arsenal of The Word, prayer, love and faith, we will win battles.

Living in Japan, we sense a tangible oppression that covers this nation. However this does not depress us, but inspires us. It is an ever-present reminder of our ever-present Hope.

PART TWO:
THE RECONCILIATION OF JAPAN
A TRUE-IN-FAITH SHORT STORY

Prologue

True faith in the Word of God means believing, beyond all doubt, that It is true and that what It says is what It means.

> "The earth is the LORD's, and everything in it, the world, and all who live in it..." Psalm 24:1

The Reconciliation of Japan is, in its most basic form—the announcement of God's desire for humankind to love without coercion, manipulation or reticence. It is the trumpeted arrival of an eternal, divine passion; the relentless pursuit of a nation's heart —a heart bound by customary restraint and guided by ghosts of the past. This reconciliation will require a definition for *what* is to be reconciled as well as clarifying the notion that something or someone *requires reconciliation*. This, in itself, points to a broken relationship and illuminates the absolute truth: ***all people are in need of a Savior.***

This is a story told by faith, so the events and details herein have not yet occurred. To understand *The Reconciliation of Japan*, we will need to displace conventional thinking to realms beyond a scientific definition of truth and the many foreknown vehicles by which truth has been demonstrated. We will need to define our version of truth according to a *divine standard*, that being Holy Scripture.

As we look into the eyes of the Japanese, we look into the souls of men and into the heart cry of God. This two-way mirror will provide answers, offer insight, and will edify the body of Jesus Christ to be assured that Japan is on its way to a mass reconciliation as seen like no other. Psalm 24 declares that the earth belongs to the Lord, and also those who live in it. But the case is not over; the evidence of faith is yet to be placed in full view for the world to examine, cross examine and rule that <u>Japan belongs to Jesus Christ alone.</u>

> *"Now faith is the subsistence of things hoped for, the evidence or conviction of things not seen"* —Hebrews 11:1

As we long for the second coming of Christ, we look to the miraculous callings, gifts, anointing and supernatural ability to serve on behalf of Christ in a Christ-less world. We proclaim our utter dependence on the Holy Spirit in order to make an ordained and eternal difference in a temporally indifferent world.

Enjoy the story.

Special Edition

The Japan Times

English version

Volume #34, Issue #301

SUNDAY, JUNE 24, 2012

NEW STATS: JAPAN 99% CHRISTIAN

"New Fire" Hits All Four Islands

It was less than one year ago that a major fire swept across the entire nation of Japan, destroying much in its path

People have been forever changed by the occurrence, many stating that they will "never be the same" since before the fire.

Centuries of ancient idol worship, Buddhist and Shinto practices have also been obliterated in the wake of this intense wave of heat.

From northernmost Hokkaido to southernmost Kyushu, nothing was left untouched by this intense, life-changing fire: The fire of the Holy Spirit.

Adults gather inside and outside of

Prime Minister to Destroy Relics

In a sweeping act of the Prime Minister and the newly-formed diet (the Japanese governmental body), all Shinto shrines and Buddhist temples throughout Japan have been destroyed by demolition followed by fire to burn the demolition remains. All

New National Anthem Instituted

Since the reconciliation of Japan, much has changed. The oppressive bondage of cultural restraint and obligation has been lifted and replaced by the very Spirit of God Himself. Public worship to God is a common practice, with the sound of praise drowning out the summer

The reconciliation of Japan is being called a "miraculous occurrence," which has garnered national media attention from around the globe. Many are in disbelief, stating that Japan has fallen prey to a mass cult, some even believing it to be the work of aliens from outer space. It continues to mystify skeptics, but has been a source of absolute encouragement for Christians around the world who are now praying for their own nations to turn to God as dramatically as Japan.

Continued on Page 4

Sundays Now Official Holidays

Most offices and small businesses have now incorporated morning prayer as a standard business

HEADLINE NEWS:
WORLD STUNNED BY JAPAN'S AMAZING CONVERSION

"But Jesus beheld them, and said unto them, With men this is impossible; but with God all things are possible." —Matthew 19:26

It was less than one year ago that a major fire swept across the entire nation of Japan, destroying much in its path. People have been forever changed by the occurrence, many stating that they will never be the same since "before the fire." Centuries of ancient idol worship, Buddhist and Shinto practices have been obliterated in the wake of this intense wave of heat. From northernmost Hokkaido to southernmost Kyushu, nothing was left untouched by this intense, life-changing fire: This was the Fire of the Holy Spirit.

In a sweeping act of the Prime Minister and the newly-formed Diet (the Japanese congress), all Shinto shrines and Buddhist temples throughout Japan have been destroyed by demolition followed by fire to burn the demolition remains. All Buddhist, Shinto and pagan religious relics, objects of ancestral worship, statues and talismans found in businesses, homes or in public places have been removed by a separate act of the Diet, encouraging people to bring these items to their local city hall for burning by incinerator.

Recycling centers have been augmented with special drive-thru areas open 24 hours to allow for the almost-continuous collection and burning of the millions of collected pagan relics. The fires burn continuously, never needing stoking or refueling because in great pleasure, God is burning it all Himself, just as He did in the days of Elijah. As long as there are objects to burn, the fire consumes.

Since the reconciliation of Japan, much has changed. The oppressive bondage of cultural restraint and obligation has been lifted and replaced by the very Spirit of God Himself. Public worship to God is a common practice, with the sound of praise drowning out the summer cicada's song. Students are often seen praying outside of their schools, joining hands together to intercede for their teachers, principals and for each other. In fact, the national motto of "Ganbatte (do your best)" has been replaced with "To God be the Glory." Even the national flag has been redesigned from the white flag and red sun to a red sun with a white cross in the center, representing Japan, the consecrated land of the "Risen Son."

The reconciliation of Japan is a miraculous occurrence, which has garnered national media attention from around the globe. Many are in disbelief, stating that Japan has fallen prey to a mass cult, still with others believing it to be the work of aliens from outer space. It continues to mystify sceptics, but has been a source of absolute encouragement for Christians around the world who are now praying for their own nations to turn to God as dramatically as Japan.

Miracles including physical healings, deliverance from emotional duress and other social dysfunctions are ever-present in Japan as the glory of God now fills the air. Families torn apart by rigid work schedules, marital affairs, domestic and alcohol abuse have been restored. Because of this, Japan's workforce has increased with great zest, bringing Japan back to the forefront of the world economy.

Children walking home from school are often found singing and glorifying God with lightened hearts, thankful for their new lives without stress and strain. Where teens and young adults used to read adult-themed manga, Bibles and the Word of God permeates the literature stands and magazine racks at 7-11, Lawson and other convenience stores.

Adults gather inside and outside of homes daily for fellowship meetings and praise festivals. Obon and other former Shinto-based religions are now banned and have been replaced with celebrations of Jesus and His anticipated coming.

On the highest mountain tops, praise can be heard for many miles in all directions. Because of this, the shrines formerly found on mountains have been replaced with special prayer stations for intercessory prayer for Japan and for other nations to come to know God in a similarly miraculous way. Shofars are blown daily from these high peaks to announce God's victory in Japan.

Former priests who had worked at shrines and temples have been retrained in the Word of God, serving as pastors all across Japan. Wedding chapels, pachinko parlors and lottery ticket sales offices have all been converted into churches, youth centers, care centers, and places of shelter in preparation for the return of Christ. Smaller facilities have been converted into Bible study centers and one-on-one counseling and prayer centers.

A national group for elderly care was created out of compassion for the millions of lonely and desperate seniors in Japan. Home care and fellowship care groups provide meals, offer prayer and assist with any needs the elderly may have. Other smaller groups have also been formed to care for individual communities and neighborhoods.

Most offices and small businesses have now incorporated morning prayer as a standard business practice, releasing employees at 5pm so they can spend quality time with their families. A national code of ethics and standards has been rewritten according to the Word of God, inspiring everyone to love each other as themselves, and to place God above all things in their lives.

This is a new Japan, reconciled to Jesus Christ Himself. A Japan which has lasted thousands of years in need of a Savior. It had been considered by many a lost nation, impossible to save as a whole because of its deeply entrenched religion and cultural strongholds. Their Savior has now arrived by His Holy Spirit, and continues to bless Japan with health, an increased birthrate, a strong economy, a reformed government with Christian leadership, and every promise seen in Scripture, given by God Himself. Amen (aka, The End).

Sounds like heaven on earth! Did you want to read more? Would you like to see this happen in our lifetime? How about in America? In any other country? Start some extreme believing. I hope that gave you a bit of cultural insight as well as how big faith can stretch—and beyond. God said he will do MORE than we could ever ask or imagine. Ephesians 3:20 tells us that He is able to do these wonderful things because of the power that WE possess through Him.

"Now to him who is able to do immeasurably more than all we ask or imagine, according to his power that is at work within us,"

This is the story in my mind's eye; my faith-mind's view of the future of Japan. I believe with all my heart that it *can* be this way. Of course I do not know what the exact future holds, but I do know that God is pleased in our worship and adoration of Him. Faith pleases Him and loving one another pleases Him because He desires our obedience along with a true relationship (John 14:15, John 15:14).

I wholeheartedly believe that we have been given great capability to *imagine things* we have never seen or heard for the purposes of faith. You can imagine someone saying something they have never said! You can imagine hearing something you have never heard! Why would we be given such gifts, to drift away in another world and be unproductive dreamers? I believe it is for purposes of believing God for the impossible.

HOW, GOD, HOW?

The Japanese are precious people. They work hard; they understand complex levels of honor and sacrifice daily in order to keep harmony and peace. In all things, the greater good is recognized far and above personal effort and reward. Unity is essential, and to do or say things that would jeopardize this cultural unity causes social strife, shame and guilt. Harmony rules.

The Japanese are known amongst themselves for their Japaneseness; their innate ability to perform, function and behave as a Japanese is expected. Japanese are raised from childhood with an array of standards, procedures, and ways of living that outsiders cannot usually reciprocate. Detail and precision are a way of life. Cleanliness and unity are touted virtues and anything less than perfect is unacceptable, however profoundly unattainable; the perfect scenario for a perfect Savior.

Because of these ideologies of how one is expected to live and operate in society, it goes without saying that they are also deeply ingrained into the minds and hearts of its people. Time-honored customs and traditions are the backbone of most Japanese today, whether they realize it or not. Attempting to function outside of these are a form of social treason; unreasonable thinking is an area upon which Japanese frown.

The most widely-known of Japanese proverbs states *"the nail that sticks up gets hammered back down."* This, in reference to social and interpersonal unity, shows the strength of the culture. No variance, much deference. But this may be the appropriate time to ask: deference to who . . . Or what?

Japan is an island nation with a 250-year history of purposed isolation, demonstrations of anti-westernization, *oneness* as a people's mantra, and unity by way of self-deprecation and suppression (of anything that may be construed as conflicting behavior with the culturally accepted norms). These, among other reasons, are likely causes as to why Christianity has not yet flourished in Japan.

Or perhaps this is result of "no demand, no supply." This is *not* to relegate the importance of Christian influence in Japan or the work being done there now by scores of local churches; quite the contrary. The Christian influence that has existed in Japan since its introduction in the 1500's (and possibly earlier) by missionary Francis Xavier has been surprisingly received—but repeatedly suppressed. During the Tokugawa period (1603-1855 A.D.), Christianity was outlawed, resulting in the execution of many Japanese Christian converts and the forced renunciation of Jesus Christ by many others.

However, by the grace and endless mercy of God for the Japanese, Christianity remains in Japan. As a light in a dark place, illuminating best where darkness is greatest.

So, we have finally come to the question by which we started this section. How, God, how? *How* can Japan be changed in such a miraculous way? With a cultural, religious and traditional backbone of iron, one that casts a shadow as large as the nation itself and covers the hearts of most Japanese today—*how* can the light of Christ break through, bringing Japan to its knees? *How* can a people so far and intentionally removed from God actually desire the God of Abraham, the love of Christ, and to be reconciled not to

Christianity alone but to Jesus Himself?

In a word, faith. But this is no ordinary word. Remember that faith is the **evidence** (proof) of things **not seen**. It starts with believing that God not only has the sovereign power to change things, but in believing that God desires to see Japan delivered from centuries of the spiritual blindness and bondage. And then finally to believe that *He will do it* according to His will and His Word.

I think many of us stop short in our faith because we may doubt what God wants or doesn't want, or we fear that we may be lacking in the details. Let me assure you, God wants *all mankind saved* (John 3:16), and He loved us enough to die in our place (Romans 5:8, John 15:13). Therefore *with all boldness and confidence you can let your heart and mind soar to places unimaginable* to most, knowing that you are indeed in God's will in prayer and asking such things (1 Timothy 2:1). We don't know the future. It is not our job to predict what God will do. Ours is to believe, to hear, and to obey.

It is through faith we do anything worth God's attention (and without faith it is impossible to please Him, Hebrews 11:6). It is by faith we move mountains of *any size*. Japan has spiritual mountains, but we can have mountain-moving faith. Believing with unwavering trust in God's ability to turn "the world upside down" (Isaiah 29:6, Acts 17:6) through Christians today as He did through the apostle Paul. In God, we are all destined to do great things, therefore anything eternity-minded is a great thing and will be rewarded (Proverbs 14:14, Psalm 58:11, 1 Corinthians 3:8, Matthew 10:42).

One hope in the writing of this book is to give you a small piece of a very big picture, but for you to take that piece and plant a seed in your heart with your own measure of faith.

The Japanese will be reconciled not by any conventional means or ideas generated by mankind. It will be through God's mercy, love and grace. And also by our faith, prayer and fasting. It will happen by the **active pursuit of such faith** and trust in the form of *actions* *which substantiate our faith* (for faith without works is dead, James 2:18, 26).

Japan is rich in many ways, powerful and intelligent. Japan may seem to have no real need for anything, including Christianity. It is through a lack of dependency on Christ and a trust in a worldly, failing system that we can see the problem. Japan exemplifies the great lie: That man can "go it alone" and be self-sufficient; that we can be a savior unto ourselves by good work or hard work. I truly believe that the *exposure of this lie* through the Holy Spirit will be experienced like the flooding of a great dam, pouring over the hearts and minds of the Japanese. It will release them into the spiritual ecstasy of *absolute liberty* and consciousness of the True God, the One and Only, Jesus Christ.

ANCIENT CHAINS

What is freedom? The Bible tells us that *"where the Spirit of the Lord is, there is freedom."* *(2 Corinthians 3:17)* Freedom, as well as bondage, can be found in many forms. Freedom is first experienced in the mind as an awakening, sensation or realization. This leads to feeling "free," released, open and unattached, fulfilled, and light. *Joy* is a counterpart to freedom. Once someone realizes they are free, that realization opens the portals of their minds to great possibilities and potential in life, regardless of physical surroundings or cultural circumstances. Sometimes this idea takes awhile as it dissolves the old fetters and shackles of bondage, to the point of understanding that only in Christ are we truly free.

The light of The Word does many things, illuminating not only the darkened areas of our lives, *but also illuminating areas we never knew existed.* This light shines into the darkened areas of our lives, showing us things that have been untouched for years and wonderful treasures within ourselves are made known. It is by His illuminating light that we are then able **to do and think** many things that were not before possible, because they were not before seen.

This next scripture shows us the mind and heart of God regarding all of us, His children:

"But you are not like that, for you are a chosen people. You are royal priests, a holy nation, <u>God's very own possession.</u> As a result, you can show others the goodness of God, for he called you out of the darkness into his wonderful light." (1 Peter 2:9)

Through the Holy Spirit of the Everlasting God, freedom will be known, and this joy and fullness will be not only illuminated, but highlighted and broadcast from the soul of every person who encounters the natural beauty of Christ's power of forgiveness —and the process of reconciliation with man's sin unto God's righteousness will be evident.

No matter how ancient or noble the tradition, or how unwavering the system of man from generation to generation, we must <u>examine the heart of all tradition and compare it to God's value system as found in the Word of God</u>. We do this to contrast it with God's definition of honor. It is by the recognition of God's honor system, and by God's value of mankind that the Japanese people will see the truth about honoring one another. Not by customary obligation, but by the grace and knowledge of what Christ has done for us that we can know how to love and honor one another.

THE LIMITLESS POWER OF FAITH

I realize I have stated these things previously, but the point must be made crystal clear: By faith God is pleased (Hebrews 11:6). Stated in the absolute obvious, when we have faith, God is pleased. When we live by the visceral as humans usually do, however, we live as the world—without Christ. We use our senses and gut reactions to determine our next move, agreeing with what is before us which limits us to the moment. In contrast, by faith we are reconciled to God and to God's *potential work*. By faith, we can move mountains, and by faith we can understand God's vision. By faith, miracles occur and by faith all things were made by and for God. By faith, men are redeemed unto salvation. By faith and the work of the faithful, Japan will know God.

We were made to worship Him in faith (John 20:29). Which is more difficult, to believe in dead spirits which do nothing but bring guilt and shame, or to honor the living Spirit of God Who enables us to live a life of fullness and joy? Japan needs the SPIRIT of the LORD. The freedom needed for this nation will grow from this cry for intimacy with a living, life-changing God.

"Preach the word! Be ready in season and out of season. **Convince**, *rebuke, exhort, with all longsuffering and teaching."* (2 Timothy 4:2)

On occasion, highlighting a statement in reverse shows completely new revelation, even thought it is simply a polarized form of the original. In this case, the scripture "faith <u>without</u> works is dead" can also be illustrated as "faith <u>with</u> works is <u>alive</u>." I prefer to use the positive end of this statement, that with faith and action, it brings forth life and newness of being.

THE KINGSHIP OF JESUS

Jesus Christ is a king. He is King over all things, all people and over all creation. He is King Jesus, King of Kings and Lord of Lords. There is no king higher, and there is no authority greater (Romans 13:1). He is not elected; he does not need a cabinet or a successor. He is Ruler Supreme who sits at the right hand of God the Father. He reigns victoriously over Satan and the demonic powers of the heavens and of the earth. He was dead but is now alive. He holds the keys of life and death in his grip. This is Jesus Christ, Savior of the world, the man who was also God in the flesh, who shed sinless blood so that we may live with Him forevermore as his kingdom servants.

Kings throughout history have typically proven their character in one of two ways. They were either productive and acted on behalf of the good of the people or they were self-serving kings, characterized by their misbehavior while on the throne of power.

The King on the throne in heaven is a good King who desires not only to have a world full of servants, but His Word tells us that for those who know him intimately, we are friends and co-laborers with whom He shares His mysteries (Deuteronomy 29:29, 1 Corinthians 2:10). He desires for us prosperity, health, wisdom, and protection. He is a loving King. Jesus calls us joint heirs of His kingdom (Romans 8:17, Ephesians 3:6). He is an intimate King who knows the names of His people (Isaiah 43:1, 49:16, Psalm 91:14, John 10:14,15).

KING OF JAPAN

Let's bring this closer to home. King Jesus created the earth and everything in it (Colossians 1:16), so how does He respond to the fact that although He may own it all, many of the earth's inhabitants do not recognize Him as King, let alone as God . . . or even as existing at all? God has a love for mankind that is like no other love. It is greater than the greatest of loves known to man, and His patience and longsuffering are deeper and wider than humankind will ever know in this life (John 3:16, 15:13).

This King does not face an identity crisis when people turn their backs on Him. He knows what He owns, and He knows who belongs to Him. He operates by the Word of His Power (Hebrews 1:3). Jesus Himself is the author and finisher of our faith (Hebrews 12:2). Faith is stronger than the mightiest foe, and wider than a vast ocean. *By faith, the people of Japan belong to Him.* By faith, the nation of Japan as a whole belongs to Him. By faith, the leaders of Japan recognize Jesus Christ and submit to His lordship. By the Word of His Power, Japan will bow its heart, bow its knee, and confesses Jesus as Lord (Isaiah 45:23, Romans 14:11).

We can speak in faith anything that is submissive to the will of God, and not contrary to His Word. In this confidence we can declare that Buddhist and Shinto shrines will no longer be visited by gift-bearing idol-worshippers, but these beautiful structures will be converted to houses of worship to the One, true God. Priests, who once practiced divination, idol-worship, and received undue offerings will repent and will direct the people to the saving knowledge of Jesus Christ.

By faith, all of this is more than possible. It is already done in the eyes of God, **awaiting our faith** to activate the blessing of this redemption. Jesus is not just King of those who bow before Him now, but He is King over all who will bow before him forevermore.

FAITH WITH WORKS IS <u>ALIVE</u>

Understanding that faith comes by hearing (Romans 10:17) is only half of the equation. **Acting upon** a given faith is the other half. Being able to demonstrate our faith through action <u>validates</u> our absolute trust in God and <u>activates</u> the faith that is "dead" without it.

Here is a simple example of faith in action. Imagine a cold, homeless man. I **believe** that if I give a man a thick, wool blanket that he will become warm. However, if I never actually **give** him the blanket, he remains cold. My *belief* is true—but followed by my *actions*, it would validate that belief. Just like that warm blanket, God's Word is full of promises that are unbreakable and absolute. There is no doubt that if we believe His Word and follow that belief with action, only great things can happen.

I am convinced that believing in something we know is right and then demonstrating our belief by acting in faith is the ultimate act of godliness. There is no work or deed that can be done which offers more merit or justification by God (James 2:23), and God is not pleased without faith. So you can see that faith is not just a good, godly principle to know and understand, but it is necessary —the lifeblood—of all works of God.

It is also necessary to note that for the perfect plan of love to operate without coercion, God needs *us* to do the work; He needs His people to be messengers for The King, and ambassadors for His kingdom. By activating our faith by speaking into the hearts and minds of the Japanese, the Spirit of God is then able to be released, penetrating even the hardest of hearts and superseding the spirit of antichrist which holds so many captive to work, money, and the empty promises of tradition.

If we believe God will heal us from a minor injury or if we believe God will change the face of Japan as we know it today, both require a measure of faith, seeing past the current situation and into the healing, into the physical change, into the heart change.

Prayer is an act of faith. Giving is an act of faith. Witnessing is an act of faith. Praising God for victory when there is no apparent cause for celebration is an act of faith; all of which are pleasing unto God.

Whether it be to change the face of a nation, to mend your marriage or to help your child in need—perhaps you have a financial burden, or a bad report from your doctor—ask yourself, "What will I do to demonstrate my faith?" What will you do to qualify the scripture, "faith without works is dead?"

Whatever you do, do *something*. And in your course of doing, believe with all of your heart, soul and mind.

PART THREE:
JAPAN MISSIONS HANDBOOK
A PRACTICAL GUIDE TO STARTING YOUR MISSIONS JOURNEY

Introduction

This handbook is a guide for those interested in or considering traveling to Japan for the purpose of missions-related work and ministry. The information presented in this book is designed to offer a basic understanding of the people, customs, and effective ministry to the Japanese in the 21st century.

As you will discover, the Japanese are a complex and globally sophisticated people. Japan ranks second only to the United States in the world economy with its export of automobiles, electronics and computer technology.

Geographical Information

Japan is an island nation, housing a massive population of 127 million. Of the entire combined land mass of Japan's four interlinked islands, only 24% of Japan is habitable due to immense mountain ranges and farmlands which span most of the country[1]. In turn, Japan is very densely populated with major metropolises boasting populations of over 12 million. Ironically, the general population is growing older with fewer women having children, thus leaving the country in an epidemic state with a rapidly dying older generation.

Despite the dramatic modernization and overcrowding of most of the country, Japan is a beautiful land inhabited by special people. Its culture is centuries old with a rich and royal history. The modern Japanese live to serve and to live according to very precise *kata*, or "ways" of doing things. The Japanese have a *kata* for doing most everything, from bathing to working and everything in between. Although the specific ways and methods of doing things are too numerous to mention, the *kata* of the Japanese makes them a mysterious and wonderful people to explore and discover.

Religious Roots

In terms of religious belief and activity, Japan is a nation of many gods and idols. *"Yao-yorozu-no-kamigami"* is translated as "a myriad of gods and deities." From the Japan Times, "A Cultural Dictionary of Japan," under the section titled "religion," *Yao-yorozu-no-kamigami* is explained as this: "Shintoism as a polytheistic religion originates with the Sun Goddess and many other mythological deities and embraces all the gods and goddesses of heaven and earth."

With Christianity comprising about 1% of the entire religious spectrum (further fragmented by denominational divide), missions work in Japan is greatly needed. Moreover, the Christian labor force in Japan is in dire need of manpower, financial support and resources to bring a saving knowledge of Jesus Christ to the masses.

Fewer and fewer American churches are sending missionaries to Japan, which means the Christian labor force in Japan is also aging, with an older generation of resident missionaries left to shoulder an incredible burden. As you read through this handbook, you are invited to pray for the nation of Japan, and pray about your involvement with Japan missions as you prepare for your trip. God will open the doors if you invite him to do so with a willing heart!

TRUE OR FALSE:

More foreigners live in Japan than any other country in the world.

False. In fact, Japan is roughly 98% homogeneously Japanese. This often makes life for English-speaking foreigners difficult as many signs, menus, instructions, documents, utility bills, etc. are not often available in English due to the relatively low numbers of English speaking people living in Japan.

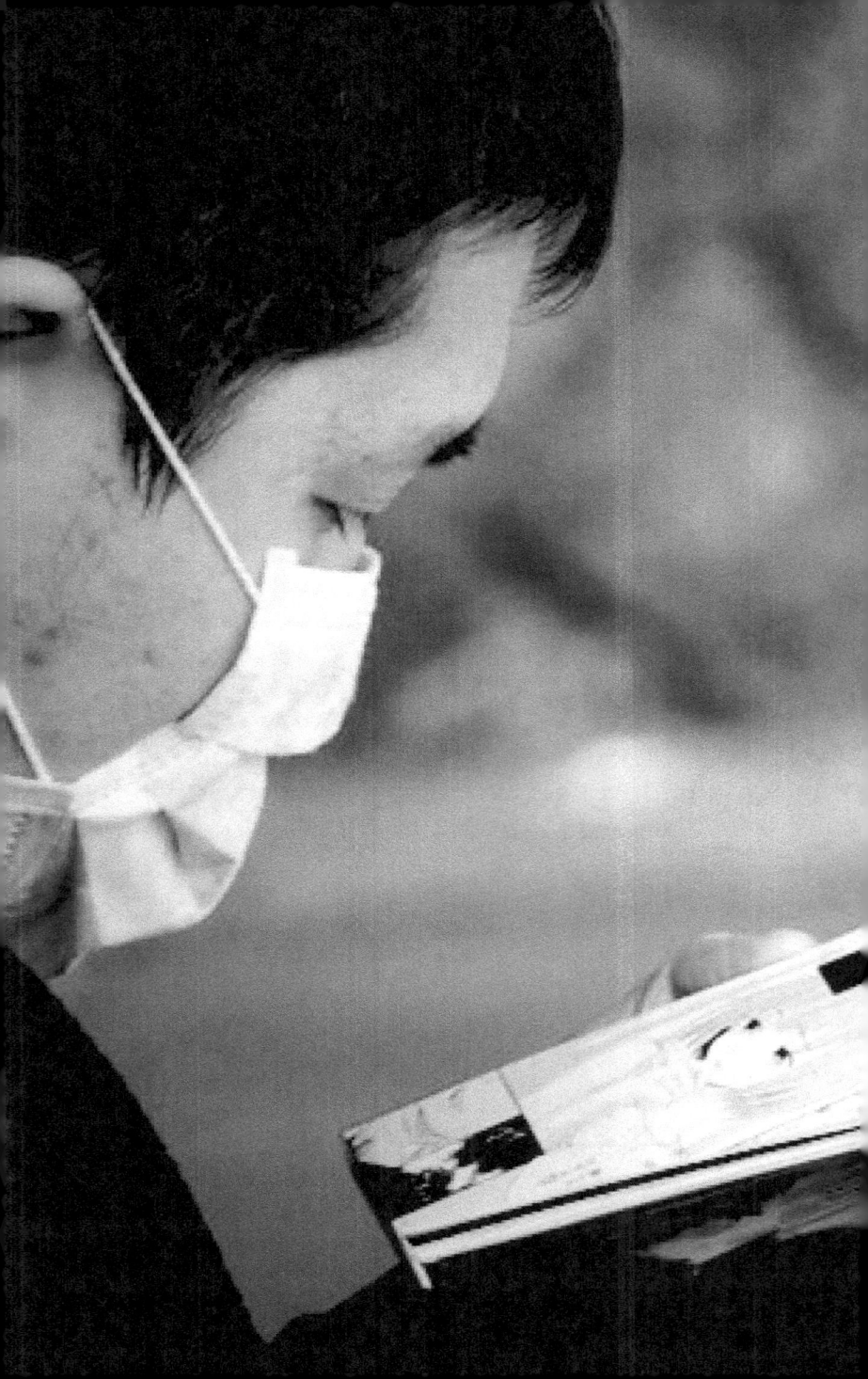

There are several key factors to consider regarding the underline culture of Japanese thinking before being able to effectively plan and execute missions work. The most important facet to remember is this: Establishing *trust* is vital. Trust is important in any relational development, especially for the Japanese. Being able to be trusted and showing your consistent loyalty and friendship will be your greatest tool in your Japanese missions ministry tool belt.

The Japanese way of thinking is one of complex structure. It is also one of great sacrifice, order, method and tradition. This is not to say the Japanese cannot appreciate the simpler points in life or are altogether restricted to speak freely; it means that what may be acceptable as free form, random or creative to a Westerner is most likely not going to be received the same way in Japan. Everyday conversation, humor, and general personal interaction are usually enunciated by way of cultural upbringing. Every action and reaction is weighted against the situation and words used. More often than not, a Japanese will take more time to answer questions, and pause between conversational segments. Body language is also very interesting. For example, many Japanese tilt their head to the side when thinking or deciding something, or may inhale through their teeth, indicating a potentially difficult situation.

Harmony Rules

The Japanese believe in the harmony of the group over individualism, and self sacrifice for the greater good of the group or community. You will learn more about this in the next section, "The Power of One & Japanese Proverbs."

The Japanese tend to avoid directness and confrontation, preferring to keep peace by way of avoiding difficult situations. While clearly communicating the gospel is the primary objective with evangelistic ministry, "guerrilla tactic" methods are not recommended. Head-on religious confrontation will only invoke walls of self-protective silence.

Displaying the love of Christ in action in Japan is a more powerful alternative, especially for short-term missions. In order to successfully relate with a love-walk mind set while being aware of the Japanese *kata*, it is important to keep patience, peace, longsuffering and time-tested consistency in the forefront of your ministry efforts.

The Bible is very clear about man's ways and thoughts: they are not like God's (Isaiah 55:8). The Japanese way of thinking is not unlike the thinking of most humans on the planet—largely humanistic (although sometimes clothed in a thin skin of religion), self-focused, and driven by work. One difference between the Japanese and Americans is in the philosophy that the greater good far outweighs individual achievement. In this, the group success often comes at the cost of sacrificing personal relationships and personal achievement.

Despite these differences, the Japanese are not unreachable—quite the contrary. They are absolutely reachable, receptive, and when affected by the love and work of Jesus Christ, they can become effective and powerful witnesses for Christianity by their own testimony. It will be your job as a missions worker to prove the scriptures by being complete in Him to do the work. By walking in the love poured out by the Holy Spirit (Romans 5:5) you will see miraculous changes over time, through prayer and consistent displays of unbroken trust.

The "Power of One" & Japanese Proverbs

This section will explain one of the most profound and fascinating points of the Japanese way of life: *The power and influence of the group*. This element of Japanese culture is embodied in every part of society, from the family unit to store workers, education systems, companies, government and beyond. The betterment of the group, team or collective unit is seen as more valuable, and is therefore the catalyst for Japanese planning and execution of ideas.

Understanding this primary motivation will enable you to better relate and function with the Japanese people. It is natural to oppose such thinking, given the oft-heard western mantras of "be all you can be," "look out for number one," and "be yourself." These ideas, although common in the west, are essentially looked down upon and are often viewed as behavior uncharacteristic of a true Japanese. Making sure the advancement of the group comes first is a key consideration.

"It Can't Be Helped"

The Japanese are largely a superstitious and proverbial society. Many live in accordance with ancient traditions, customs and sayings, whether they realize it or not. One of the most disparaging of sayings still uttered today is "shikata ga nai (仕方がない)." This means "It can't be helped." It is a potently negative statement which is used when there seems to be no hope of change or alternative for the better.

A famous proverb which demonstrates the group mentality as previously described is "Deru kugi wa utareru (出る釘は打たれる)." This means "The nail that sticks up gets hammered down." This proverb is perhaps one of the most detrimental since it is a widely known and practiced philosophy which is deeply rooted into the culture today. Getting past the traditional rhetoric and examining it in light of scriptural truth will be a challenge, but also a tremendous blessing when the truth comes to light. Trusting in the guiding power of the Holy Spirit will make the difference in your ministry approach.

Becoming a Christian in a historically Buddhist/Shinto religious culture would certainly be cause to be labeled as a "nail sticking up." Given the Japanese are keenly aware of this mentality, "sticking up" is not something anyone really desires to do—at least not for very long.

In a fashionable and trendy part of Tokyo known as Harujuku, young people dress in wild costumes representing a variety of themes from Gothic Lolita to Anime characters. Prehaps they are dressing to impress or to shock, almost in anti-establishment style as was seen in the early punk rock movement of the late 70's in England and the United States. There is an outlet for expression here which goes beyond the norm, and could very well be construed as a public display of the need for uniqueness. Because Japan is so homogeneous on many levels, uniqueness is easily spotted and therefore goes against the general flow of Japanese group culture.

The conformist mentality and the stigmas of ancient traditional proverbs and attitudes can be overcome by faith, prayer and spiritual warfare against wickedness in high places; a bondage which holds millions of Japanese captive to the past. Everyone desires to feel wanted, loved, and to know that they are special. Identity through Jesus will break this bondage.

FACT OR FICTION:

Tokyo is the largest city in the world.

True. Tokyo boasts the largest metropolitan population of over 35,000,000 people.

A Brief History of Christianity in Japan

Several books and personal writings have been collected on the subject of Christianity in Japan, from the 16th century to today. Inasmuch, Christianity is not new to Japan, but has seen a volatile rise and fall over the past 460 years or so.

Laying the Foundation

In the year 1542, the first Europeans from Portugal landed on Kyushu in southwestern Japan. Earnest missions work began in 1549, led by Francis Xavier, a Portuguese Jesuit priest. Up to the year 1600, the founding Catholic missions work in Japan was carried out by 95 Jesuits. Some were Portuguese, Spanish, and Italian. A few of the early Japanese converts were also instrumental in assisting the work of the Jesuits. The Japanese barons on Kyushu welcomed foreign trade, especially because of the new weapons, and therefore tolerated the Jesuit missionaries. The missionaries were successful in converting large numbers of people in western Japan including members of the ruling class.

In 1550, Francis Xavier undertook an unsuccessful trip to the capital Kyoto, spending 11 days ministering. With compounded difficulty and lack of willingness for those in Kyoto to hear the gospel, Xavier and his fellow brothers in the faith returned to their work in Kyushu.

Christianity Loses Ground

Towards the end of the 16th century, the Jesuits lost their monopoly position in Japan when Franciscan missionaries arrived in Kyoto despite a first banning edict by daimyo Toyotomi Hideyoshi. In 1597, Hideyoshi proclaimed a more serious banning edict and executed 26 Franciscans in Nagasaki as a warning. Tokugawa Ieyasu and his successors continued the persecution of Christianity in several further edicts. As many as 280,000 Japanese Christians were persecuted and thousands were martyred.

In 1626, Christianity was banned in Japan and for the next 250 years, Japan closed its doors to the rest of the world.[2]

The Doors are Reopened

It was only in the mid-1800s, when Commodore Perry of the US Navy forced Japan into signing an agreement that caused Japan's isolation to come to an end and trade with the rest of the world.

In 1859, the first seven Protestant missionaries arrived in Japan.

In 1868, Emperor Meiji worked hard to modernize Japan, importing the latest technology and foreign talents from the West. Japan also sought expansion throughout most of Asia. The defeat of Japan in World War II marks the first time in history when Japan suffered defeat and occupation by a foreign power. Japan was compelled to adopt a democratic constitution (thus ensuring religious freedom), renounce war and ban State Shinto (Emperor worship).[3]

21st Century Missions

Today, one to two million Japanese are Christians (about 1% of Japan's population). Most of them live in western Japan where the missionaries' activities were greatest during the 16th century.

As the world economy has changed dramatically in the 21st century, church emphasis on world missions has diminished. The reduction in sponsored missions work has led to the decrease of active missionaries in many countries, not excluding Japan. Those who were or have been sponsored are growing old, retired, having served for decades with fewer new missionaries being sent.

The need for missions work in Japan is great, and the need for workers who can dedicate their time and energies is immense. The western Christian influence is helpful in Japan and offers support to keep the Japanese church from being "hammered down" culturally, driven back to conformity in terms of religious views. Thankfully among Christians, many denominations set aside their differences for joint events and services carried out in the name of Jesus Christ.

Throughout history, Japan has repeatedly rejected Christianity because of suspicion of this outside/non-Japanese influence. While the Christian doctrine should not be adjusted to suit the Japanese temperament, much can be done to help Japanese own the Christian faith for themselves by incorporating more of their traditions into their faith and to worship God in their own distinctively Japanese ways.

HISTORY:

Catholic Jesuit Francisco Xavier landed on the western shores of Japan in 1549. A museum dedicated to the early history of Japanese Christianity can be found in Nagasaki at the *26 Martyrs Museum.*

The Japanese Christian Church Today

Today churches in Japan remain relatively small, with an average attendance of 10 to 30 people attending Sundays. Some exceptions include churches in larger metropolitan areas. The majority of these in attendance are women. Sundays are the only day off for most men, who usually spend these precious days off relaxing or participating in family activities.

Christians are a very small minority in a largely agnostic society where consensus is important, and because of this, individuals who have decided to become Christians can often feel exposed and vulnerable, especially in their own homes. Even Christian families face pressures from their communities. Cultural pressures to conform can come in the form of an obligation to participate in religious festivals and rituals, ancestral worship and in helping to take care of the local shrine.

Munakata Bethel Christian Center's international congregation.

Although this may seem bleak in terms of potential for growth, today's modern church in Japan—such as Munakata Bethel Christian Center—is a vibrant, Spirit-filled body which seeks to serve God with an earnest heart, and with an upright attitude. Worship services are joyful, with congregants displaying meekness of spirit and integrity in the Word. It is a true joy and pleasure to serve there.

Education for kids is high priority and is taken very seriously. Young people are often seen in uniform whether in or out of school. Clubs and after school activities, followed by "juku," prep school usually leaves the student on their way home around 9 or 10 pm, and often later. Because of this, reaching students is a difficult task which requires prayer and wisdom from above. The students are usually open to the gospel . . . They just need time and opportunity to hear it!

Practical Ministry

Knowing little of the Japanese language, and perhaps even less about the culture, you may be wondering . . . "How can I effectively minister to the Japanese people?"

Don't Worry

The first step in making this journey successful is simple: don't worry! Leave your anxieties and cares to the Lord. As you begin to trust the Lord in this area, the Holy Spirit will enable you to do the work He intends for you to do. Do not try to anticipate "how" God will use you; be yourself and serve your leadership with a willing heart.

What will show itself true to the Japanese is your genuineness of spirit, and your willingness to serve. Have joy and peace as you minister to people who need the love and liberty of Jesus Christ.

Second, remember that even though the Japanese may live differently, look and act differently than what you are used to, they are people just like you and me. Keeping this in mind, you will find ways to truly relate and connect, making your missions experience one you can be sure made a difference!

Ministry Opportunities

Japan offers unique opportunities for Christian ministry. Since Japan is predominantly non-Christian, it is clear that there are many who have never before heard the gospel of Jesus Christ. Therefore, there are many who have never witnessed the kind of love that only God can reveal. And certainly, there are many who have never before received a genuine touch from a living, active God.

Many have never experienced or seen healing, and many are

oppressed of the devil and demonic forces. There are many opportunities which are sure to change and affect lives. Be of good cheer! Because of the sheer numbers of people living in Japan, you may feel as though you are only making a minor difference, or that the work you are doing could not possibly cause a lasting affect. If God's Word is used for ministry, it will make a difference no matter how great of an outreach, or how intimate of a personal connection.

"So shall My word be that goes forth from My mouth; It shall not return to Me void, But it shall accomplish what I please, And it shall prosper in the thing for which I sent it." (Isaiah 55:11)

Remember to keep the cause of Christ in your sights at all times, despite the occasional overwhelming of the senses and the potential for frustration due to cultural differences. Use all of the gifts and abilities that God has given to you. Be yourself, and minister in the ways that God leads either personally or through your leadership.

Pray

Jesus understood the will of his Father because he was in constant prayer and communion with Him. You should do the same! Being in a foreign country can be cause for fear and stress due to questions and are uncertainty of your every move. Pray through your times of difficulty, leaning on the One who knows exactly how to reach the people of Japan.

Don't let the "work" supersede your dependency upon the Holy Spirit to work through you. God has brought you to this place in life—receive it with His blessing and do well!

Language and Customs

Take a Bow

A primary custom is seen in greetings and acknowledgements in the form of the common bow, called "ojigi." The bow is the Japanese way to greet, confirm, thank, and bid farewell. Bowing is used for almost everything. Bowing is usually used in place of a handshake or a hug, although some are comfortable with bodily contact.

Formal bows are deep bows from the waist, with hands at the side (for men, hands in front for women), while the daily bow to a friend or store worker may be a small nod of the head. Verbal greetings are also quite customary, depending upon the situation and those involved.

In slightly more formal situations, the exchange of name cards is still widely practiced in Japan. Have your own name cards handy (I would reccomend one side English, the other Japanese).

Alphabet Soup

One of the most difficult barriers to overcome in any foreign country is the native language, both spoken and written. Japan is no different in that much of its written language is derived from native Chinese characters which have been further translated into the Japanese education system and everyday reading and speaking.

The Japanese use two syllabaries: *Hiragana* is the native Japanese character set. *Katakana* is used when writing or speaking of things which are non-Japanese in origin; along with *Kanji*, symbols adopted from Chinese which indicate meanings per symbol rather than sounds per symbol as with Hiragana and Katakana. Even fluent Japanese speakers often struggle with Kanji because there are many thousands of characters which can be learned, with multiple meanings and sounds for a single kanji character.

An Inside Look at Japanese Language

Every language has its rules of speech, and Japanese is no different. Japanese is easier than English in some regards, but more difficult in others. The sounds you hear in the Japanese alphabets are always pronounced the same way, with no exceptions. The sound for "wa" will always be pronounced "wa." This can be said of every symbol in that they do not change with the surrounding text, as may often be the case in English. For example, "<u>ch</u>ocolate" and "<u>ch</u>iropractor."

Another interesting facet is how to turn a statement into a question. This is accomplished in its most basic form by adding the sound "ka" at the end of the question. Read more about this in the next few pages.

I understand is pronounced, "Wa-ka-ri-masu."
Do you understand is pronounced, "Wa-ka-ri-masu-ka?"

Basic Language Tips: Pronunciation

In this section you will be able to read and speak a few Japanese words. You will see these examples written in what is called "Romaji," a phonetic translation of the word shown, using the English alphabet. The basic Romaji vowel sounds are as follows:

A	as in "f**a**ther"
I	as in "**e**ach"
U	as in "s**u**it"
E	as in "**e**cho"
O	as in "**o**pen"

Consonants are never spoken together, sounds such as TR, PL, BR, etc. which makes English often difficult for Japanese to master complex pronunciation. The word "steak," for example, then becomes, "su-te-ki," written in *katakana* (phonetic) form.

Basic Language Tips: Phrases

Some of the more common phrases you may hear include:

	My name is ___ .
Hello.	**Watashi no namae wa ___ desu.**
Konnichiwa.	
	I'm sorry.
Good morning.	**Gomen-nasai.**
Ohayou gozaimasu.	
	Nice to meet you.
Good night (to sleep)	**Hajimemashite.**
Oyasumi nasai.	
	Goodbye. (long-term)
Excuse me.	**Sayounara.**
Sumimasen.	
	Please. (request)
Where is the toilet?	**Onegai shimasu.**
Toire wa doko desu ka?	
	Goodbye. (informal)
What is your name?	**Sore dewa.**
O-namae wa nan desu ka?	
	Please. (offer)
How are you?	**Douzo.**
O-genki desu ka?	
	I don't understand.
Fine, thank you.	**Wakarimasen.**
Genki desu.	
	Thank you [very much].
Yes.	**Doumo arigato [gozaimasu].**
Hai.	
	I can't speak Japanese [well].
No.	**Nihongo [yoku] hanasemasen.**
Iie.	
	Do you speak English?
Is there someone who speaks English?	**Eigo o hanashimasuka?**
Dareka eigo o hanasemasuka?	

"Christian" Phrases in Japanese*

Below are some phrases which might be familiar to you as a Christian. These are everyday phrases and words you may want to know and reference in your work with the Japanese.

-- I would like to pray for you. Will you agree with me?
Anata no tame ni inoritai desu kedo, yoroshii desu ka?

-- God bless you.
Kami-sama no shukufuku ga yutakani arimasu youni.

-- Jesus is the same yesterday, today and forever.
Iesu Kirisuto, kinou mo, kyou mo, itsumade mo, onaji desu.

-- The Bible is true. You can be certain of this.
Tashika ni, seisho wa shinjitsu de arimasu. (or, **shinjitsu desu.**)

-- God, thank you for everything.
Kami-sama, subete no koto wo kansha shimasu.

--I am a Christian.
(Watashi wa) kurisuchan desu.

-- Would you like to know about Jesus Christ?
Iesu Kirisuto ni tsuite, motto shiritai desu ka?

*Note: Many words in Japanese end with the sound "u" although it is sometimes not pronounced audibly, such as the word "desu" which means "it is." The phonetic pronunciation would sound more like "dess." The "u" sound can be said, however, and would not be improper if spoken, but in most common conversation is left out.

Question words usually end with the sound "ka?" with an upward voice inflection to emphasize the question. Most Japanese is spoken very evenly with no breaks or dramatic movement in rhythm. Japanese text is written with no spaces between words. Periods are seen as a small circle, called a "maru" or "ten."

Fast Facts

Shoes are never worn in Japanese homes and in some restaurants.

Chopsticks are usually used when eating, but western tableware such as forks, spoons and knives are usually available upon request. In the event that tableware is not available, practice using chopsticks (before you arrive in Japan)!

Slurping your food is acceptable and normal, but never blow your nose in public. It is considered unhealthy. Sniffing, however, is completely acceptable.

Money is not usually exchanged hand-to-hand in stores or restaurants. Small money trays are provided for giving and receiving money.

Gift-giving is very important in Japan. Be prepared to give small gifts, usually a local craft or item from your area. There are many complexities in honor that come along with gift-giving.

Bow appropriately. Deeper bows for deeper respect and first meetings. Small nods for casual acknowledgements.

Do not wear shoes or your guest slippers in home restrooms. Toilet room slippers are usually provided.

Many Japanese toilets are heated, some even with a bidet installed. Most Japanese public rest room stalls go all the way to the floor for privacy. Toilet seats may also include sound effects or music for modesty.

Traditional Japanese toilets are essentially ceramic holes in the floor with a flush handle. These are subtly referred to as "squatters." Watch your balance and don't get your pants wet!

Hugging, kissing and sometimes hand-holding are viewed as public displays of affection which are typically not seen (usually viewed as erotic in nature to older generations). However these days you may see people holding hands in public while walking, but kissing in public is very much reserved for intimate moments in private.

Social Issues

Japanese life is based around large-scale concepts of harmony, order, tradition and honor. You will find components of these primary elements in most everything in Japan from office etiquette to grocery store layouts. The kata of everyday life consists of those things which bring and keep harmony, dissuade conflict, and display outward control and order.

Stores are meticulously dressed. The smallest of packages are beautifully wrapped, and employees of companies large and small are expected to function to keep harmony in the group. The way things are done in Japan is essential to the success of being Japanese and in understanding the Japanese.

Religion is important in Japanese culture, both nationally and individually. Religious activities are usually conducted as a family, but infrequently. Moreover traditional religion is often viewed simply as "culture," not separated from the individual or seen specifically as spiritual. Family obligation of the first-born son demands that honor and respect is given to the family's dead ancestors. This, in turn, requires the family to manicure graves, submit offerings and prayers, and commit themselves to lifelong honor in many traditionally religious ways. *Death is one area of Japanese life where religion and culture are bonded very tightly.*

The Japanese are, in the sincerest respects, bound by the details and commitments of their own culture. Working long and hard hours prohibits most fathers from having any sense of a "normal" existence, rarely seeing their wives and children. Religious activity and commitment keeps families bound to ancient traditions and respect for long-dead ancestors.

Another element of life in Japan concerns the family. The Japanese business man or "salaryman" works an average of 10 hour days, and are often expected to socialize until late, returning home after 10 pm. The wife is expected to care for the family, and to tend to her late-arriving husband.

Things are slowly changing in Japan with regard to dysfunction in the family unit, but only after decades of divorce, abortion, child suicides and intolerable stress levels seen in all age ranges from grade school into adulthood. Younger generations seem less interested in the ways of history or tradition.

Marriage in Japan is often a very practical institution. Older married couples do not tend to display public affection. Many married couples do not use the words "I love you" or have never said them to each other.

Mothers are the caregivers and nurturers of every day needs. Fathers are the breadwinners. Many marriages exist today with epidemic problems facing the younger generation such as the indulgence of marital affairs, lack of communication with their spouse and family, and an overall sense of duty rather than a love-filled relationship.

Illicit sexual behavior is widespread in Japan by way of pornography and the use of "love hotels" where married affairs take place every day, all over Japan.

Food, Vending Machines & Money

Japanese foods are interesting and fun to try! You will want to explore Japan's cuisine culture, despite what you may think you know or perceive about Japanese cooking. Food in Japan is fresh, often colorful and delightful to eat.

Seafood - Hundreds of different fish, shellfish and other seafood from the oceans, seas, lakes and rivers are used in the Japanese cuisine. They are prepared and eaten in many different ways, for example, raw, dried, boiled, grilled, deep fried or steamed. Commonly prepared seafood includes sashimi, sushi, and yakizakana.

Noodles - There are various traditional Japanese noodle dishes as well as some dishes which were introduced to Japan (and subsequently Japanized). Many of them enjoy a very high popularity. Common noodle dishes in Japan are soba, udon, ramen, somen and yakisoba.

Rice - For over 2000 years, rice has been the most important food in Japanese cuisine. Despite changes in eating patterns over the last few decades and slowly decreasing rice consumption in recent years, rice remains one of the most important ingredients in Japan today, and can be found in numerous dishes such as the common rice bowl, sushi, onegiri, dombori, kare raisu, fried rice, chazuke, and okayu.

Nabe - Nabe dishes or hot pot dishes are prepared in a hot pot, usually at the table. Typical ingredients are vegetables such as negi (Japanese onion) and hakusai (Chinese cabbage), various mushrooms, seafood and/or meat. Some special nabe dishes are: oden, sukiyaki, and shabu-shabu (Japanese-style fondue with meat and soup).

Sweets - Japanese sweets are called wa-gashi in Japanese, and western-style sweets are called yo-gashi. Common ingredients for wa-gashi are rice flour, azuki (red beans), and sugar. Butter and milk are rarely used in wa-gashi cooking, so wa-gashi tends to be lower in fat than yo-gashi. Wa-gashi can be very sweet, so it goes well with strong green tea. Some common sweets include manju, anmitsu, ohagi and daifuku.[4]

Vending Machines

Vending machines in Japan are not only popular, but they are found everywhere and can contain just about anything such as soda, beer, food, condoms, ice cream, batteries, toys, razors, hot beverages, tobacco and even clothing. Japan is a nation full of small wonders, such as these ever-present vending machines, which are usually clean, in proper working order and well-lit. Some now even include a localized wi-fi signal.

Convenience stores are also very popular. On most any street one can find a 7-11, Lawson, am-pm, Circle K, Poplar, or a Family Mart. These stores are termed *"konbini,"* which is shortened slang for "convenience."

Money

Unlike America, Japan is very much a cash-based society. Japanese currency is counted in Yen, pronounced "En." Currently, Japan uses three different denominations of bills, and six types of coins, shown here. Counting and converting money can be a bit daunting at first due to the higher numbers used with Yen versus the American dollar. Before you spend money, but sure you understand the value you are spending. Smart phone applications are available to help convert.

Japan is a land of commercial spending, full of stores and shopping to accommodate every whim and need. Money is very important both in the realm of commerce and religion, as money is often used as a gift to leave as an offering at temples and shrines.

What NOT to Do in Japan

This section details a few of the things you will want to remember while in Japan, primarily what not to do when in the company of others. As Japan is honor-centric in many ways, it is important to "do as the Japanese do" especially while establishing new friendships and trust. It would be advisable for you to memorize this simple phrase in Japanese: *"Go ni ireba, go ni shitagae."* This is an invaluable expression. It comes from the proverbial expression which means, *"When in Rome, do as the Romans do."*

Many times Japanese will tell a first-timer to Japan, "Oh, you use chopsticks so well!" So in context of this example, a visitor could reply with a smile, *"Go ni ireba, go ni shitagatte imasu,"* meaning "I am doing in Japan as the Japanese do." Host family members will be thoroughly impressed.

I think most Japanese display a fairly positive disposition, but this may very well be what Americans know as a "poker face." In Japan, it is called "Tatemae." Outwardly you may see smiles and agreeance, but inside might be a different story. You will most likely not be corrected, but actions which yell "foreigner" are likely to stick with a slightly negative impression.

• Do not argue with a police officer, especially if you do not speak Japanese. Like most nations in the world, there is on occasion a sense of discrimination and bias against foreigners. Arguing with police may cost more than you are willing to pay in time, money and hassle.

• It is better to decline an evening of karaoke and social drinking than to act stand-offish later on while in the midst of your company. The latter will only cause offense and confusion about why you are present to begin with.

• Do not put your chopsticks in or on a community serving bowl full of food.

• Do not point at people with your chopsticks or set your chopsticks on the side of your own dish. Use your chopstick holders.

• Do not show overt public affection, even to your own spouse. You may be tempted to offer your own sense of "liberty" by showing your affection publicly, but this will only work against you as many find public affection offensive and something reserved for an intimate setting.

• Avoid introductory situations without bearing a gift. The Japanese are very keen on gift-giving and certain elements of such giving must be present in order to be received properly. The size and value of the gift is important, so be careful not to shop too cheaply and not too lavishly on a first meeting.

• If you have tattoos, you might want to keep them covered in public. Although you may not be Japanese, the Yakuza (Japanese gangsters) are well known for displaying their large tattoos as a symbol of power and gang affiliation. Recently, especially for foreigners, tattoos are becoming more widely accepted, but it is still rare in Japan. You will also avoid unnecessary run-ins with police if you keep your tattoos under wraps.

• Do not walk around a Japanese home with your shoes on. They should be removed at the entrance after you enter. The front door area is called the *genkan*. It is common to see rows or piles of shoes here. Your host may provide a pair of slippers for you for general use and a separate pair for the rest room.

Trip Checklist

You will want to bring with you several items to Japan. Please use this trip checklist as a guide to remembering the essentials.

1. Your Bible, bilingual version if you have one.

2. Money to change to Japanese Yen (¥). Bring your US dollars with you, but have some yen handy for airports, taxis, etc. You will more likely get a better rate converting in Japan.

3. This book (just in case).

4. Notebook and pens/pencils for notes and journaling.

5. Shoes that slip on and off easily (you will take off your shoes in all Japanese homes) such as Crocs® brand shoes or similar.

6. Small gift items (new, wrapped) from your local area to give to hosts and people you will meet.

7. Photos of your family. Sharing your life with others in an intimate way is a big part of ministry.

8. If you plan to travel, a guidebook with maps and tips for dining, sightseeing, etc. would be helpful.

9. Summer months in Japan are extremely hot and humid in most of Japan. Be prepared for it by bringing light clothing. Winter months are cold, and Japan does not have central air or heat, so dress in layers.

10. Your camera. Don't miss an opportunity to snap a shot of new friends or the beautiful scenery in Japan.

Praying for Japan

The prayer of faith is the greatest need for Japan. You should pray as you are led for the people of Japan, but here are some specific suggestions which might help to guide you.

• Pray that God will shake the nation overall, to cause a great awakening to the knowledge of Jesus Christ. (Hebrews 12:28)

• Pray that marriages will blossom into loving relationships where family supersedes ancestral past, growing closer than ever before. (1 Peter 3:1, 7)

• Pray that the false face of religion will be exposed and that spiritual darkness would be removed from Japan. (2 Timothy 3:5)

• Pray that the sexual depravity of Japan will be broken, and that men and women will reconcile their marriages unto God as He is made known to them. (1 Corinthians 6:18)

• Pray that the ministers currently in Japan are provided with needed resources, financial support and moral support. (1 Timothy 5:17)

• Pray that more churches in America would respond to the needs of ministry in Japan to affect the masses. (James 5:16)

• Pray that God would send more workers to Japan so that Japanese missions can be accomplished with larger vision and a stronger, younger workforce. (Mark 16:15)

PART FOUR (A):
RELOCATING ABROAD
TIPS, ADVICE AND PROCEDURES FOR MOVING OVERSEAS

Are you called to a country and a people which is not your own? Have you heard from God regarding missions work and are ready to take the "plunge" in your faith walk?

If that is you or if you are on the edge of what you feel is God's leading into full-time missions work, the next section will be very helpful to you.

It contains tips, advice and procedures to get yourself, your home, and your paperwork in order. The preparation for moving abroad is a somewhat daunting process, and the reality of leaving your home behind or selling all that you have for the sake of others is indeed scriptural, but the reality setting in can be overwhelming if you don't have a roadmap to help you through the process.

I hope this next session continues to bless and inform you. My first piece of advice for you, the one whom God is calling as He did Abraham, "Go from your country, your people and your father's household to the land I will show you." (Genesis 12:1) is this:

Keep your spiritual ears open

Once you make your decisions and goals public, people will naturally want to offer you advice, and it may be good advice. But in a case such as moving abroad for spiritual reasons, trust only the leading of the Lord. If you are married, be sensitive to your spouse as big moves usually involve big stress. Don't give place to the enemy for breaking apart a new work of the Lord in your hearts by keeping your ear inclined to the Holy Spirit.

Keep your focus clear

"The steps of a good man are ordered by the Lord: and he delighteth in his way." (Psalm 37:23)

If you don't have the "whole picture" from God yet, wait until you know what to do next. That does not mean knowing all of the details, it means wait until you know what to do next.

Genesis 6:13   God told Noah why he was going to end humanity.
Genesis 6:14   God told Noah to prepare by building an ark.
Genesis 6:15   God told him how to build it.

Noah built the ark based on what God told him, not what he *thought* was a good thing to do. But Noah he did not get all of the pieces at one time. It was a very long process from the call to build, to the time of the flood. Theologians estimate that it took Noah anywhere from 55-75 years to build the ark.

Abraham, on the other hand, was called to go, but given not much else until he arrived in country. Abram was seventy-five years old when he set out from Harran. Noah was 600 when the flood came.

Given these two examples, take this to heart: God is not in a hurry, but He wants to to act according to His timeline for your life. It might take years to get there (read our testimony starting on p. 13), but press in and press on.

Go with a blessing from your local church

Blessing and honor go hand in hand. When we receive blessings from God, He, in turn, receives honor through our lives.

I believe Noah's success came because of what he did as seen in Genesis 6:22: *"Noah did everything just as God commanded him."*

Obedience is a wonderful and marvelous thing. Hear the call, but obey the voice of God. Do what is right, and don't take shortcuts.

Much is the same in terms of receiving a blessing, or in being "sent off" by your ordained pastor. The blessing of being "sent" also includes the blessing of your congregation, and hopefully their support in prayer, encouragement and finances.

Blessings are to be given, not taken. Hopefully you would have spoken to your pastor about your intent to move abroad by the time you make actual arrangments to do so. Having the blessing of your church will take you leaps and years of effort ahead of going it alone. If your church practices the laying on of hands, I would strongly recommend asking your pastor if he or she would bless you in this way. Biblically, it has great meaning and historically, both Old and New Testaments describe various situations where the laying on of hands was done. Primarily it was to separate, or to remove from the group. To consecrate, make holy or set apart for a special task or work.

Its significance can be evaluated in connection with four concepts: *blessing, miraculous power, separation,* and *the coming of the Holy Spirit.*

> This "formed at an early period a part of the ceremony observed on the appointment and consecration of persons to high and holy undertakings;" (and in the Christian Church was especially <u>used in setting apart men to the ministry and to other holy offices. It is a symbolical act expressing the imparting of spiritual authority and power.</u> --ED.)[5]

and furthermore,

> There is a sense in which the idea of separation for a special purpose, so clearly visible in many instances, binds together all the occurrences of the phrase. Even in the context of formal

blessings and astonishing miracles, the imposition of hands signifies the separation of a person, a people, or even a bodily part (Mark 8:25) as the recipient of an unusual manifestation of God's grace. --Frank Thielman[6]

Raise awareness

It is vital that others in your family, your friends and those in your home church are aware of your intention to move abroad into full time ministry. Increasingly, people are leaving churches for too often the wrong reasons. To avoid any miscommunication, be sure your goals are clear, and that you convey to as many people as possible your plans, timing and needs.

Use Facebook®, Twitter®, your own website, any means possible to announce what you are doing. Be clear and direct in your statements, and keep it simple.

Create a newsletter right off the bat using any popular newsletter/ mass email programs such as MailChimp®, Constant Contact® or iContact®. Gaining some traction by way of a mailing list will help you significantly in the future. People can always opt out or unsubscribe later if they like.

Raise funding

It is difficult to estimate what it might cost for you to move overseas, but with plane tickets, shipping, and general expenses to re-establish ourselves cost our family of four about $20,000.00. We were blessed to pay very little of that amount ourselves, as it came in by way of special donations from our church congregation and family members who were able to support the initial move. You may not need this much money, or you may need more. Being able to clearly state your needs will help significantly. For example, if someone asks you, "what is your greatest need right now?" Rather than being modest and saying, "well we need a lot, but God knows our needs," which is true, you might want to consider a more direct response, such as "we need plane tickets, and they cost such-and-such amount." I might follow it up with, "if you know of anyone who might be inclined to know more or help, please let them know."

The absolute truth is, God *does* know your needs, but He often fulfills them through people. So by stating your needs both to God and to others, you are acting in accordance with your own faith (*working* your faith) and prayers, seeking God for His help to move on the hearts of men to provide for you.

Inasmuch, ongoing fundraising will be imperative to your longevity, so starting a newsletter long before you leave is one of the best pieces of advice I can give you regarding travel preparations. Keeping people abreast means keeping you in their minds and in their hearts. I heard that a missionary to Sweden once said,

"I was told that when I became a missionary and left home, I would be forgotten in six months. I was very sad by this news, but even moreso surprised when it only took two."

I chuckled when I first heard this, but when a similar reality came to life in our own situation, it wasn't so funny. We did not keep up as much as we should have with communication. The first few months were so grueling and tiresome, energy was being expended in every way, especially mentally. New language to learn, paperwork, physically moving things, etc. It was very taxing. If we had stayed up on the communication through this process (it will be hard, but do it!), we may have had fewer "drop offs" and more support in all ways. Live and learn. I lived, you learn.

Travel light

When we departed for Japan we brought only what we thought we needed, but it turned out to be three pallets of "stuff." Most of it was books and our kids' toys. We were told by our senior missionaries that furniture was too costly to ship due to weight. Not only that, American furniture is huge in contrast to Japanese furniture. This is because homes are generally smaller with smaller spaces to fill.

So unless you are aware of your future home and its storage options, space, etc. I would highly recommend bringing only the essentials and perhaps some things that make home feel like "home" such as your favorite Christmas decorations, photos, and special momentos. Everything you bring with you will add to your shipping costs, so choose carefully. Also, traveling light will keep your focus sharp, and will give you a better chance to "start clean," buying what you need rather that what you may be burdened with in the end.

Debt

I hope this one is obvious enough. Clear all debt before you go. You will have more than enough to be concerned with in your efforts to reestablish yourself abroad. The last thing you need is a creditor contacting missionary so-and-so for an old bill. Not only does that add financial stress, but it also makes for a bad witness. Your income may or many not be affected once you make the move to missionary status, but my guess is you will make less unless you have a really amazing support chain. I pray that you do. Anyway, leave with a clean slate. Do your best to have as little debt as possible.

Paperwork

Early on, this will be a process and it seems unending for awhile. However, I hope this description of the process mixed with some advice will give you a clear picture, and smooth sailing as you move forward.

First, if you are coming to Japan to live, you cannot simply move to Japan with a suitcase and your guitar on your back. You need valid proof of your intent to work under the guidelines (restrictions) of a Religious Visa, proof of income and backing from a sponsor who already lives in Japan. This is where communication and networking will work with your faith. You do your part, God will do His.

Your sponsor will need to vouch for your ministry work and will be used sort of as an agent or proxy to ensure that you are truly coming to Japan (or wherever you are headed) for the purposes by which you stated on your forms. This puts your proxy in a bit of a place of responsibility, should anything go wrong in the future. Please keep this in mind as a common courtesy and as a good witness.

The next page or two is taken directly from the US State Department website, which details the process and procedure for obtaining a temporary overseas religious activities visa. Should you have questions on this information or process, you can visit the website directly, or contact them via the information provided on the website.

Starting Your Visa

Hold onto your hat, and don't get discouraged! The following process may appear more intimidating than it really is.

The following information is from the US State Department:
http://travel.state.gov/content/visas/english/other/religious.html

Obtaining a Temporary Religious Worker Visa

As a Temporary Religious Worker, You Must:

be a member of the same religious denomination as the religious organization you plan to work for in the United States for at least two years before that organization files a petition on your behalf;
be coming to work as a minister or in a religious vocation or occupation in the United States;
be employed by a non-profit religious organization in the United States (or an organization affiliated with the religious denomination

in the United States); and work at least part time, an average of at least 20 hours per week.

For Some Temporary Religious Activity, a Visitor (B) Visa Can Be Used

Certain religious related activities can be undertaken using a visitor (B) visa, such as private worship, prayer, meditation, informal religious study, and attendance at religious services or conferences in the United States. Also, a visitor visa is generally appropriate for ministers of religion seeking to come to the United States temporarily, whose wages and reimbursement will be paid by their own religious group outside the United States, and when coming for:

An evangelical tour, without taking an appointment with any one church; or
Exchanging pulpits temporarily with U.S. counterparts; orMembers performing missionary or
voluntary service for a denomination, such as to aid the elderly or needy.

When you have a religious vocation or profession, or are a religious worker coming temporarily to be employed, with your salary paid by a non-profit religious organization in the United States, the visitor visa is not permitted, and you must have a religious worker (R) visa or other work visa.

Petition Approval

Before you can apply for a temporary religious worker visa at a U.S. Embassy or Consulate, a Petition for a Nonimmigrant Worker, Form I-129, must be filed on your behalf by a prospective employer and approved by U.S. Citizenship and Immigration Services (USCIS). For more information about the petition process and eligibility requirements, see Working in the U.S., Temporary (Nonimmigrant)

Workers, and R-1 Temporary Nonimmigrant Religious Workers on the USCIS website. USCIS will notify your prospective employer about the petition approval or denial, by sending a Notice of Action, Form I-797.

How to Apply

There are several steps to apply for a visa. The order of these steps and how you complete them may vary at the U.S. Embassy or Consulate where you apply. Please consult the instructions available on the embassy or consulate website where you will apply.

Complete the Online Visa Application

Online Nonimmigrant Visa Application, Form DS-160 - Learn moreabout completing the DS-160. You must: 1) complete the online visa application and 2) print the application form confirmation page to bring to your interview. See official State Department website to apply online.

Photo - You will upload your photo while completing the online Form DS-160. Your photo must be in the format explained in the Photograph Requirements.

Schedule an Interview

While interviews are generally not required for applicants of certain ages outlined below, consular officers have the discretion to require an interview of any applicant, regardless of age.

If you are age 13 and younger then an interview is generally not required. 14-79 Required (some exceptions for renewals)
80 and older generally not required

You must schedule an appointment for your visa interview, generally, at the U.S. embassy or consulate in the country where you live. You may schedule your interview at any U.S. Embassy or Consulate, but be aware that it may be difficult to qualify for a visa outside of your place of permanent residence.

Wait times for interview appointments vary by location, season, and visa category, so you should apply for your visa early. Review the interview wait time for the location where you will apply:

You must provide the receipt number printed on your approved Petition for a Nonimmigrant Worker, Form I-129, or Notice of Action, Form I-797, to schedule an interview.

Prepare for Your Interview

Fees - Pay the non-refundable visa application fee, if you are required to pay it before your interview. When your visa is approved, you may also pay a visa issuance fee, if applicable to your nationality.

Gather Required Documentation

Gather and prepare the following required documents before your visa interview:

Passport valid for travel to the United States - Your passport must be valid for at least six months beyond your period of stay in the United States (unless exempt by country-specific agreements). If more than one person is included in your passport, each person who needs a visa must submit a separate application.

Nonimmigrant Visa Application, Form DS-160 confirmation page. Application fee payment receipt, if you are required to pay before your interview.
Photo - You will upload your photo while completing the online Form DS-160. If the photo upload fails, you must bring one printed photo in the format explained in the Photograph Requirements.
Receipt Number for your approved petition as it appears on your

Petition for a Nonimmigrant Worker, Form I-129, or Notice of Action, Form I-797, from USCIS.

Additional Documentation May Be Required

Review the instructions for how to apply for a visa on the website of theembassy or consulate where you will apply. Additional documents may be requested to establish if you are qualified.

Attend Your Visa Interview

During your visa interview, a consular officer will determine whether you are qualified to receive a visa, and if so, which visa category is appropriate based on your purpose of travel. You will need to establish that you meet the requirements under U.S. law to receive the category of visa for which you are applying.

Ink-free, digital fingerprint scans will be taken as part of your application process. They are usually taken during your interview, but this varies based on location.

After your visa interview, your application may require further administrative processing. You will be informed by the consular officer if further processing is necessary for your application.

When the visa is approved, you may pay a visa issuance fee if applicable to your nationality, and will be informed how your passport with visa will be returned to you. Review the visa processing time, to learn how soon your passport with visa will generally be ready for pick-up or delivery by the courier.

Important Additional Information

Petition approval by USCIS does not guarantee visa issuance.

Do not make final travel plans or buy tickets until you have a visa issued and in your possession.

Unless canceled or revoked, a visa is valid until its expiration date. Therefore, a valid U.S. visa in an expired passport is still valid. If you have a valid visa in your expired passport, do not remove it from your expired passport. You may use your valid visa in your expired passport along with a new valid passport for travel and admission to the United States.

Spouse and Children

Your spouse and unmarried children under age 21 may apply for R-2 visas to accompany or join you to reside temporarily. You must demonstrate that you will be able to financially support your family in the United States. They are permitted to study while in the United States, but are not authorized to accept employment.

For information about employment or stud while in the United States, review Religious (R) Workers and Employment Authorization on the USCIS website.

PART FOUR (B):
GETTING SETTLED ABROAD
TIPS, ADVICE AND PROCEDURES FOR PLANTING YOUR ROOTS

First months abroad: I just want to sleep!

From our experience, the first few months after arriving in Japan were definitively the most difficult physically and mentally. We were told this might happen. It was like a months-long jetlag but with more drastic effects.

We were drained and wanted to sleep all the time. For three months, this feeling lingered. We had so much on our minds, so little we knew, and depended heavily on our sponsoring missionaries. They called us several times a day, asking if we needed anything or support. They were awesome! I pray one day I can do the same for someone else (maybe you!). I felt very comforted by the fact that they would help us if we needed it.

The first few months required establishing our home. We could not read or understand much Japanese at that time, so even small things became cumbersome and stressful, such as pumping gas (voice-prompted in Japanese), figuring out Japanese currency, reading signs, reading our mail (was it important or junk mail?), setting up utilities, etc. The list was long.

All that to say, the first few months are full of ups and downs. You are *up* and excited because FINALLY you are in that special place where God brought you, but *down* because you are human and big moves take a big toll on your senses. *Up* because we were now full time ministers excited to do God's work, but then *down* because we didn't know how to communicate with anyone! It was a lot of emotional tug-of-war, but time heals, time helps, and time still aids us in communicating the love of God as much as possible.

Becoming a foreign resident

Since we arrived in Japan, the process for becoming a resident has changed. Please note that becoming a resident does not mean you are a citizen of Japan. You will not have the right to vote or participate in government. Only if you become a naturalized citizen of Japan (by the way, Japan does not allow dual-citizenship; you would have to forfeit your status as an American citizen in order to receive Japanese status) will your rights extend only slightly above being a resident. Many do not find it worth it to fully commit to citizenship by way of naturalization.

Given the process has changed, here are a few guidelines as detailed on http://japan-guide.com. These guidelines are for both non-permanent and permanent residents of Japan.

Alien registration

The Alien Registration system was discontinued on July 9, 2012. Instead, foreigners are now registered in the same residence system as Japanese nationals, and alien registration cards are replaced by residence cards (see below). Old alien registration cards can be used instead of a residence cards until they expire or until July 8, 2015, whichever comes first.

Residence Card

As of July 9, 2012, all new foreign residents are issued a residence card upon initially entering Japan at Narita, Haneda, Kansai or Chubu Airports. New residents arriving through different ports can get their cards at their municipal offices. Existing residents may continue to use their alien registration cards instead of a residence card until their cards expire or until July 8, 2015, whichever comes first. At that time, their alien registration card will be replaced by a residence card.

The residence card is an important document required for opening a bank account, obtaining a cell phone, converting a drivers license and similar activities. It stores the holder's personal information, including the current address, the status of residence and period of stay. Foreign residents are required to carry their residence card with them at all times.

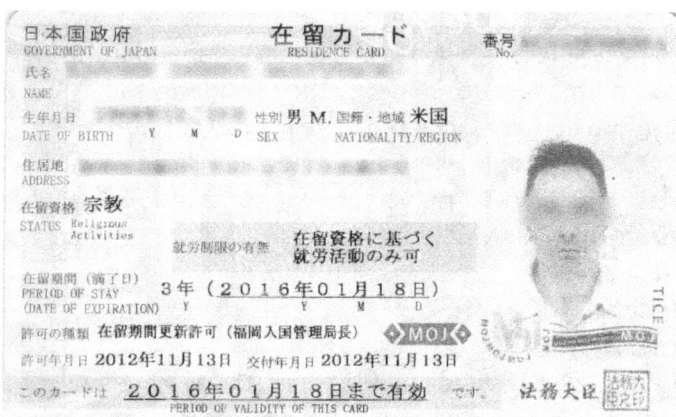

Extending residence permission

Most statuses of residence allow you to stay in Japan for a period between three months and five years. If you wish to stay longer, you must apply for an extension at an immigration bureau inside Japan before the expiry date of your current residence permission.

The application process is relatively simple, provided that you still fulfill the conditions for the specific status of residence. It typically takes a couple of days or weeks for the application to be processed, and you are allowed to remain in Japan during that time even if your previous residence permission expires in the meantime.

Changing status of residence

It is possible to change your status of residence (e.g. from temporary visitor to instructor or from student to engineer) at an immigration bureau inside Japan. You will have to provide similar documentation as you would have to when applying at an embassy or consulate outside of Japan.

Permanent residency

Foreign residents who have shown good conduct and have sufficient assets or ability to make an independent living, can be granted permanent residence if they reside in Japan for typically ten or more consecutive years (less in case of spouses of Japanese nationals and people who have made significant contributions to Japanese society). Permanent residence status is indefinite and allows any paid activity.

Naturalization

Foreigners, who have resided in Japan for at least five consecutive years (less if married to a Japanese national), have shown good conduct, have never plotted against the Japanese government, have sufficient assets or ability to make an independent living and are willing to renounce any other citizenship held, can be granted Japanese citizenship.

Driving in Japan

You may wish to get a drivers licence while living in Japan. From our experience, it was helpful for more than just driving. Without it, we were not able to contract for a cell phone, and having another official form of ID is always a plus. This section will help you to understand the ins and outs of getting a license. As you may read from various blogs on the web, preparing and testing for your license in Japan is not for the easily discouraged. Most foreigners fail multiple times before actually passing the test, which is done on a closed course.

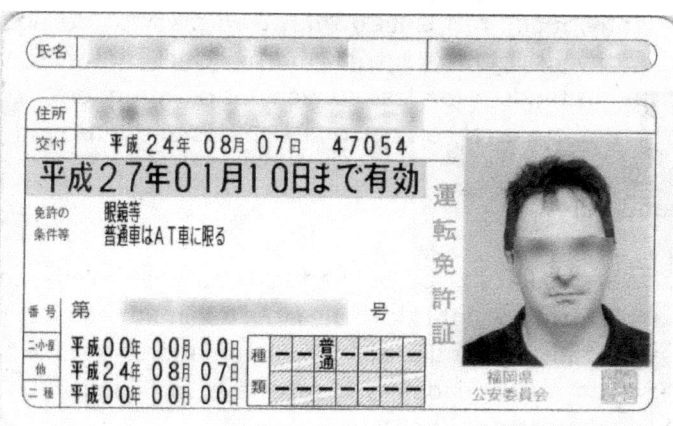

Japanese drivers license. A green stripe means a standard license status. A gold stripe indicates being accident free for 5 or more years.

Japanese road signs.

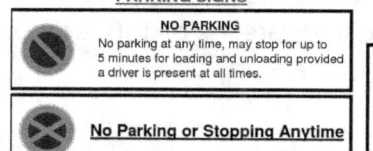

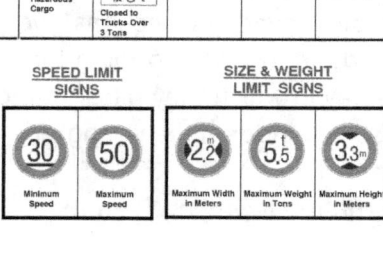

Japan's large metropolitan areas around Tokyo, Osaka and Nagoya are served by highly efficient public transportation systems. Consequently, many residents do not own a car or do not even possess a driver's license. Outside the big cities, however, public transportation tends to be less convenient or infrequent, so most people in rural areas rely on personal vehicles to get around.

Roads and Rules

Cars drive on the left side of the road and have the driver's seat and steering wheel on the right side. The legal minimum age for driving is 18 years. Road signs and rules follow international standards, and most signs on major roads are in Japanese and English. Drinking and driving is strictly prohibited.

The typical speed limits are 80 to 100 km/h on expressways, 40 km/h in urban areas, 30 km/h in side streets and 50 to 60 km/h elsewhere; however, drivers tend to go a little over the posted speed limits.

Most roads in Japan are toll free with the exception of expressways and some scenic driving routes. Road conditions tend to be good, although side streets in the cities can be rather narrow or even impassable to larger vehicles. Traffic congestion is a frequent problem in and around urban centers.

Drivers generally tend to be well mannered and considerate, however some common dangers on Japanese roads include drivers speeding over intersections even well after the traffic light has turned red, people stopping their vehicles at the edge of the road in a way in which they block traffic, and careless cyclists, especially those who ride on the wrong side of the road.

International Driving Permits

Foreigners can drive in Japan with an International Driving Permit

(IDP) for a maximum of one year, even if the IDP is valid for a longer period. It is not possible to drive on an International Driving Permit again unless you return to your home country for at least three consecutive months in between.

International driving permits are not issued in Japan and should be obtained in your home country in advance. They are usually issued through your country's national automobile association for a small fee. Japan only recognizes international driving permits based on the 1949 Geneva Convention, which are issued by a large number of countries.

Belgium, France, Germany, Monaco, Slovenia, Switzerland and Taiwan do not issue permits based on the 1949 Geneva Convention, but instead have a separate agreement that allows drivers from these countries to drive in Japan for up to one year with an official Japanese translation of their driver's license. A translation can be obtained from the Japan Automobile Federation (JAF) or some of the respective countries' embassies or consulates in Japan.

People from other countries whose international driving permits are not recognized by Japan and people who stay in Japan for more than one year, must obtain a Japanese driver's license.

Japanese Driver's Licenses

Japan has bilateral agreements with more than twenty countries, including Austria, Australia, Belgium, Canada, the Czech Republic, Denmark, Finland, France, Germany, Greece, Iceland, Ireland, Italy, the Netherlands, New Zealand, Norway, Portugal, Slovenia, South Korea, Spain, Sweden, Switzerland, Taiwan and the United Kingdom, to ease the process of acquiring a Japanese license. If you hold a valid driver's license from one of these countries, you can get a Japanese license without taking a written or practical exam.

Drivers test course

Instead, go to your local license center with an official translation of your license (obtainable from JAF), your passport, and proof that you held your license for *at least three months in the issuing country before coming to Japan*. Then, take a basic eye and physical test and you will be issued a new license on the same day.

If you have a driver's license from a country which does not have an agreement with Japan, such as the United States, China or Brazil, you will have to take a written and practical exam in order to obtain a Japanese driver's license. This process typically takes several attempts, even for experienced drivers.

Buying and Owning a Car

New and used cars are relatively inexpensive in the home country of Toyota, Nissan, Honda and Mazda. Brand new compact cars sell for less than a million yen.

Japanese cars are classified into regular and light (keisha) cars, which are subject to different taxes and regulations. Keisha cars (yellow license plates) are smaller vehicles that must conform to strict size, weight and power restrictions. In return, they enjoy several tax and toll breaks, and relaxed ownership regulations that make them cheaper and easier to own than regular cars (white license plates).

Owning and operating a car involves numerous expenses, including compulsory inspections (shaken) every two to three years, yearly automobile taxes, mandatory and optional insurance, high parking fees, toll expressways and gasoline cost.

Shaken is a compulsory safety inspection, which cars in Japan have to undergo every two years, except new cars, for which the first inspection is not due until three years after purchase. Shaken typically costs between 100,000 and 200,000 yen, and besides the actual inspection fee, includes a weight tax (typically 8,000 to 50,000 yen) and mandatory insurance (about 30,000 yen).

Since the mandatory insurance does not provide full coverage, it is recommended to purchase additional, secondary car insurance. Furthermore, the annual automobile tax, which depends on the engine size, typically costs between 10,000 and 50,000 yen. An acquisition tax also has to be paid when you buy a new car.

Numerous documents are required to purchase a car, including forms to register your car and to verify ownership of a parking space. Used cars additionally requires a transfer of ownership. Keisha cars enjoy more relaxed transfer processes. Fortunately, if you buy a car through a car dealer, they will handle most of the paperwork for you, while your main task is to sign the forms with your officially registered, personal stamp (inkan).

Smaller keisha have yellow license plates, while regular sized cars have white license plates.

Gas Stations

Gas stations in Japan traditionally provide full service, although self service stations have greatly increased over recent years. Many gas stations close during the night, while others are open 24 hours. A liter of regular gasoline costs roughly 150 yen (as of March 2014). High octane gas and diesel are also widely available. Payment is possible by credit card or cash.

Getting gas at a full service (フル) station requires some simple Japanese. When you pull into the station, an attendant may direct

you to a stall. Park, open your window and shut off your car. Tell the attendant what kind of gas (e.g. "regular"), how much (e.g. "mantan" for full tank) and how you will pay (e.g. "credit card"). He may give you a wet towel to clean your dash or ask to take your garbage. When finished he may ask which direction you wish to leave and then direct you out into traffic.

Self service (セルフ) stations only provide Japanese language menus. If in trouble, an attendant should be present and able to help you. Note that when paying by cash, the change machine is often a separate machine or inside the gas station building.

Parking

Parking in the center of large cities is very expensive, costing several hundreds of yen per hour. Fees decrease with the size of the city and the distance to the city center. In small towns and in the countryside, parking is often free. Parking lots in national parks or near tourist attractions sometimes charge a flat fee (typically 200 to 500 yen per use). Urban hotels usually provide parking for their guests at a flat rate (typically 1000 yen per night), while hotels outside the large cities usually offer free parking.

Besides standard parking lots, you may encounter a few unique types of parking lots in Japan. The first are elevator parking lots in which cars are stored in towers. Drivers are directed to park their car onto a lift, which will automatically store the car in the tower. When coming back, the car will be fetched by the lift and returned to you.

The second unique type of parking lot uses low barriers underneath the cars which raise up to physically block in each individual vehicle. Once you have paid your parking fee (either at a central payment machine or at the parking space), the barrier lowers and you can safely drive away. This type of parking lot is usually seen around small urban lots.[7]

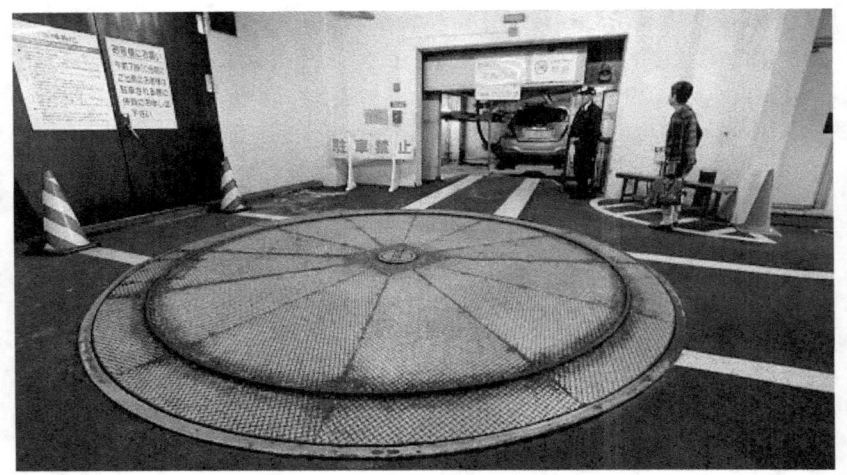

Housing/Finding an Apartment

Whereas apartments are measured in square feet in the US or identified by rooms (1-bedroom, 2-bedroom, etc.), the measuring system is different in Japan. Both apartments and single-family homes are measured using a *tatami mat system*. A tatami mat is:
1) traditional Japanese rice straw mats used as flooring material.
2) used as an expression of measurement for property and homes.

A tatami mat measures approximately 3ft by 6ft (18 square feet) or approximately .9m by 1.8m. Tatami mat measurements can vary from region to region, but sizes are generally similar.

When looking for housing, you will see the abbreviations for apartments listed as LK, 1K, 2K, 1DK, 2DK, 1LDK, 2LDK, etc.

The first number refers to the number of bedrooms, D stands for Dining Room, L stands for living room, and K stands for kitchen. Although "living, dining, and kitchen" are English words, this is one area where western culture has influenced Japan. In the US we use slightly different terminology, but the general idea is the same:
BR (bedroom), B (bath), LR (living room), K (kitchen), 1/2 bath (bathroom with a toilet and sink, but no shower).

Apartments are usually rented through real estate agents rather than directly through property landlords. Real estate offices can be recognized by listings of available apartments in their show windows. They also advertise on signs in the neighborhood and in various publications.

Conventional Real Estate Companies

The rental system of many conventional real estate companies is *not* very foreigner friendly.

Apartments are usually rented for a minimum of two years, which conflicts with the fact that many foreigners stay in Japan for less than two years. Furthermore, many landlords are reluctant to rent their apartments to foreigners who are not able to communicate in Japanese. Some of them will even categorically refuse their service to non permanent residents out of fear of frictions.

You will be required to have a guarantor co-sign the rental contract as another security measure. Certain conditions apply as who can serve as your guarantor. It *must be a Japanese national* with a stable financial background.

Entering a rental contract with a conventional real estate company is expensive. A number of refundable and non-refundable fees have to be paid, often totaling three to ten months' rent, depending on the company and apartment:

Reservation fee (tetsukekin)
The tetsukekin is paid when you apply for an apartment, and before the actual rental contract is signed. It serves as a guarantee for you that the apartment is not given to somebody else, and for the agent that you do not change your mind. It is refunded after the actual contract is signed and is usually equivalent to about one month's rent.

Deposit (shikikin)
The deposit is used to cover eventual future damage to the apartment. The deposit minus the cost for repairs is refunded when you move out. The deposit is usually equivalent to several months' rent.

Key money (reikin)
This is a non refundable payment to the landlord in the amount of up to several months' rent.

Service fee (chukai tesuryo)
This is a non refundable payment to the real estate agent in the amount of at most one month's rent.

In most cases, apartments come unfurnished, utilities are not included in the rent, and pets are not allowed. Please read more about Japanese apartments and furniture.

Real Estate Companies for Foreigners

Real estate companies, which specifically target Japan's foreign community, exist mainly in Tokyo and other large metropolitan areas. They offer private and shared apartments for conditions that are much more suitable to the needs of foreigners, and often have staff trained in foreign languages.

Many real estate companies for foreigners operate so called gaijin houses ("foreigner houses"), a very inexpensive type of accommodation, while others target individuals and businesses on larger budgets and with higher requirements.[8]

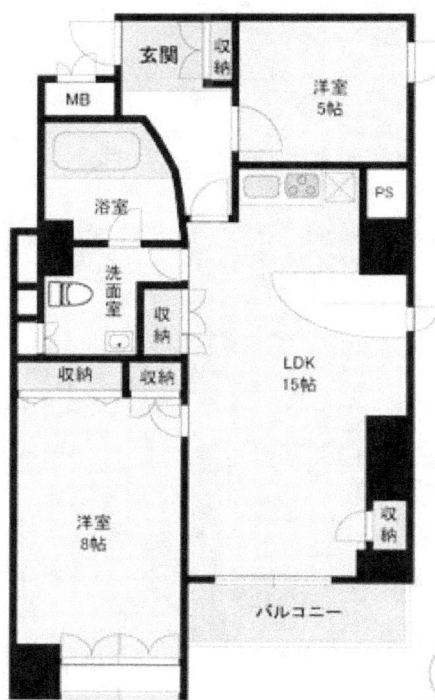

A Typical 2LDK

玄関 (genkan)
- entrance

浴室 (yokushitsu)
- bathroom

洗面質 (senmenshitsu)
- washroom

洋室 (yoshitsu)
- western-style room

収納 (shuuno)
- storage/closet

8帖 (hachi-jo)
- 8-tatami (size)

バルコニー (barokonii)
- balcony

押入 (osiire)
- closet

物入 (monoire)
- cupboard

居間 (ima)
- living room

N

PART FIVE:
FINAL THOUGHTS

In this section we will briefly explore these topics:

- EDUCATION OPTIONS FOR CHILDREN
- KEEPING SPIRITUALLY FIT
- EMBRACING THE CULTURE
- A DAY IN THE LIFE . . . WHAT TO EXPECT

Education Options in Japan

There are many considerations regarding your children's education when moving to Japan. The first would be to consider their age, and what their education options would be at that age. Essentially, there are three options, all with pros and cons.

Home school

From those we have known abroad, this is often a missionary's typical route, provided one of the parents is able to teach full time. Home school is perhaps the least expensive option of the three we will explore, but it has a number of elements which should be considered equally. Depending on your level of financial support or arrangements you may have with your sending church or agency, home schooling may or may not be the best option.

Home school kids often face issues of isolation, loneliness and boredom because of the lack of interaction with peers and people outside the home. Our kids faced these things at various times, but in the end, it was the best choice for our family for a number of reasons. You will also have to make the choice of whether or not home school is feasible.

Some of the pros of home schooling are that your kids will not need to learn a foreign language at the same time they are schooling, although it is highly recommended. Being able to communicate is key to making relationships, and subsequently, friends. Another positive aspect is that it can much more deeply grow the relationship between children and parents. It is also a generally safer idea since it does not involve travel or the kids being alone, however Japan is considered a very safe country with a very low crime rate. At a school, however, bullying can be an area of contention. Unless your kids are emotionally prepared for things such as peer pressure, bullying and struggling through school in another language, it might be best to consider home school.

Another benefit of home school is flexibility. If your kids were to attend Japanese public school, they would have to leave very early, and would quite possibly not be home until after 4 or 5 pm. The Japanese school system is based on the idea of working hard, embracing your school, and actively participating on all levels. As we discussed earlier, the group benefit is not to be compromised, even at very early levels of education in Japan.

International Private School

This option is for those who can afford it (the closest international school to us costs about $20,000 US dollars each year per student), and for those who live near a major metropolis which provides such schooling. Benefits of international school are that your child will be exposed to various teachers, trips, and resources that home school cannot usually provide. Classes are also taught in English. However, unless you live in the same city as the school, your kids would be required to take a train or some other form of public transportation each day. This means letting go of the parental reigns a little bit, trusting God to keep your kids safe.

Japanese Public School

This is perhaps the bravest option of all, but if your kids were either born or raised knowing Japanese, this may possibly be one of the better options for you since communication would not be a major issue. Mom or dad does not have to teach with this option, and the kids would have plenty of peers to keep them company. However, they would need to conform very heavily to the Japanese school system, which is very strict compared to US (and possibly other western countries) standards.

For example, as in most Japanese homes, Japanese public schools do not have central air or central heating systems, so extreme months of hot and cold weather can be challenging. Also, public schools do not hire janitors to clean the school. The students are required to clean their own classrooms, restrooms and hallways. This is meant to build respect for their school and to help students develop a good work ethic early on.

From jr. high through high school, uniforms are required to be worn. They must be privately purchased by the parents at special stores which sell school uniforms, and can become costly, usually over $100 US dollars per set which includes winter wear, summer wear and physical fitness uniform. Restrictions on hairstyles will also most likely apply. Hair may not be dyed, earrings may not be worn and nail polish may not be used. Uniformity of appearance is a key factor in Japanese public school.

Japanese public school is very competetive because from jr. high to high school, a test must be taken to enter high school (only through jr. high is education required). Better schools require higher test scores, so preparation is a big deal since much pressure comes from parents as well as peers. The "jukus" or preparatory schools, are full until late into the night with students preparing to enter high school or college.

Japanese school, however, will probably yield the most friendships between the other options, so if social needs are important to your child, this might be one option to consider.

Japanese elementary school. Uniforms are not required until jr. high.

Japanese high school classroom. Kids do not use lockers since the students stay in class and the teachers rotate. It is very efficient for the sake of time spent.

School trip. All are required to stay in a group, and of course are in uniform.

Typical Japanese school uniforms. Kids are often seen wearing uniforms even on weekends and holidays, and usually until late at night.

Keeping Spiritually Fit

Keeping oneself spiritually fed can be a challenge, especially if you are in a position where most everything falls on your shoulders. Services, music, outreach, relationships, etc. -- having a schedule that is too big will cause one to lose sight of "feeding" themselves spiritually.

A tired body and a tired mind cannot last very long, and certainly cannot study the Word, study Japanese and raise a family all at the same time. I am speaking from experience when I say that keeping yourself spiritually in tune with God, making time for prayer, Bible reading and personal moments of worship are perhaps the greatest challenges on the mission field, but also the most imperative.

Time with God

You will have to MAKE the time. Make it a decided factor in your ministy life. Ministry work will certainly not carve out the time for you, because there is always more to do in a day than we can squeeze in, but we always try. You will have to set some boundaries and make your personal time with God key, whether it be every morning or some other time of the day.

I recommend mornings for Bible reading and/or devotionals. Evenings can easily get away if projects or meetings go long, and before you know it the process has repeated itself for a much longer than expected period. This will leave you dry and tired, and over some years without proper spiritual support, you may end up qutting prematurely. Prepare and press on! <u>Dig in with a strategy!</u>

Following a strategy is how wars are won, both physically and spiritually. How you keep yourself in spiritual shape is just as important as physical shape. Trust me, I know! I live it every day and the challenge never becomes less important or any easier. However, the decisions as to what and how to do that are always in my court, so as a father of two teens, keeping my wife and kids spiritually fit is also a high priority. We all do our best, and we try to motivate each other. The culture of Japan (and every country) has its own challenges and strongholds. For Japan the greatest stronghold in my opinion is the culture of conformity. It makes for being a Christian difficult if one is not truly "sold out" for Christ, and may lead to a compromising lifestyle. This leads to my last point in this section.

Embracing the Culture

Since Japan is largely non-Christian but is in fact open to Christian ideas, there is great opportunity here mixed with great challenges.

Embracing the culture of the people, as mentioned in **Part Three** of this book, is key to making your life a wonderful thing in Japan. Embracing and trying to understand the culture will also aid your evangelistic efforts. Our senior missionary is an avid student of Chinese kanji and its origins. He often uses illustrations of kanji, broken down in parts, to examine scripture or to make a point based on the language of Japanese itself. It is often eye-opening and a wonder to the Japanese how this foreigner could be so astute in a language not his own. It is nothing short of God's own creativity which helps to bridge the cultural gaps.

Be wise in your approach to the non-Christian culture of Japan. Our first target should always be the hearts of the Japanese, to use the love of God to reach out. Once God gets ahold of people's hearts, their minds will become transformed by their exposure to the Word of God (Romans 12:2). We pray daily for various friends, neighbors, people in our community for opportunities to share the love of God with them. We make relationships with anyone we can including our local gas station attendants, grocery store clerks, teachers, sales people who come to our door including the local Jehovah's Witnesses. If they are open to the truth, that is all that counts! If not, we have done our part and we move on.

A Day in the Life: What to Expect

Sometimes differences in things we are used to may be a bit frustrating and take some time to get used to them. We have found that Japan has many conveniences that are found in other industrialized nations, but many things are quite different.

First and foremost, cash vs. checks. Japan is largely a cash-based society, with no PIN-based debit cards used. Credit cards are generally accepted, but Japanese credit cards can only be used for purchases where the repayment terms are set in advance, such as one payment, two, or three (generally). The payments are then deducted automatically from your bank. Personal checks are not used in Japan.

You can easily pay your bills electronically. When you sign up with the utility companies, they ask for your banking information. This is so that when your notice arrives that the bill will be due soon, you can prepare by having enough money in your account to cover the amount. It is deducted automatically.

The Japan Postal system is unique in that it is also a bank. So while you are shipping packages, etc. you can have the fees deducted from your account. You can also easily transfer money to another person using the JP Bank ATM. It is very convenient and the Japan Post office service is second to none, in my opinion.

Japan is a world-class exporter of electronic goods, the leader in the robotics industry, and ranks highly in education. But Japan is also a very *manual* country, meaning many things are "do-it-yourself." For example, most homes do not have garbage disposals, but rather use small net bags inside of the sink drain which are emptied daily.

Doing laundry is especially tasking because in Japan electric dryers are generally not used, nor are they generally sold in any appliance stores. Most homes and apartments use only a washer with a high-speed spin cycle which dries the clothes fairly well. After that, they are hung inside or outside on lines to dry. Japan's cityscapes are all lined with laundry lines, especially in the summer months. Because there are relatively no dryers, during rainy and cold seasons many people use a "wash house," which is essentially a laundromat with mostly dryers.

Japan does not use central air or central heat in most homes, and is often not found in many older public buildings and offices. That means summers can be brutally hot and winters can be very cold. The systems most people use is an air conditioner/heating unit that are installed in each desired room. Often, only one unit is being run at a time for energy conservation, so the household members gather in the room where the cool/hot air is found. Many do not use the air conditioners at night for fear of catching colds and to save electricity. If you stay in a host home, depending on the season, you may experience a bit of discomfort if you are unable to communcate your preferences.

Grocery shopping is an experience Tracy and I enjoy because the speed of life in our area (and in many areas across Japan) is much slower than that of a bigger city. The aisles and displays are always pristine, and people move rather slowly through the store. I have yet to see any form of public commotion or a real outburst in Japan. It happens, but it is rare. Although the world is changing even in Japan, the idea of harmony still exists and is evident.

In most towns, walking and bike riding is a very normal way to get around. Especially prevalent are small scooters, driven by anyone from teens to senior citizens. Because people do a lot of walking and by way of cultural rebirth through the education system, most value exercise and keep exercise as a part of their lifelong routine. Only 3% of Japanese are considered obese in contrast to the USA at 34%, taken from a 2013 study by the World Health Organization. Most people are slim with smaller body types, so if you are a larger person, try not to feel self-conscious. The Japanese do not expect you to look Japanese :)

The Japanese are eco-friendly and do their utmost by recycling anything that can be recycled, such as batteries, lightbulbs, newspapers, cans, bottles, plastic, etc. Recycling centers are always crowded with lines of cars waiting to dispose of their recyclable goods.

All in all, Japan is a great place to live and we love living here. The people are good-natured, careful and honest. Crime rates in Japan are very low, and work ethics are strong. Great attention to detail and supreme customer service are the norms, from hotels to McDonald's you will always receive courtesy and respect.

Of couse everyone's life is different, so a "day in the life" for you will be based on the choices you make and how you decide to live your life abroad. We have decided as a family to keep things simple, to keep our costs low so that when we have time to spend together as a family, we can do things such as go out to eat, see a movie once in awhile or just relax at the ocean with a bento (box) lunch.

Whether you move to Japan or another country abroad, get used to the customs of your "host" nation, and embrace them! Enjoy being among the people and share your own culture with them. It will be a mutually satisfying time of your life, so savor the moments, treasure your relationships and do your best to make the most of every moment.

Each day is a learning experience, and an opportunity to challenge ourselves in our faith. God never lets us down, nor will He let you down if you are ready to step into your future. We are excited for you!

Final (*Final*) Thoughts and . . .

Thank you.

You took the time to read this book, and if you made it to this page, you now know many things you may not have before. I pray that it has enriched your understanding.

This information may have inspired you, or perhaps it made you nervous. My hope is that even though this book is packed full of little tips, advice and information, that it boosts your faith to believe God for more. Living life in another country and reading a book about it and are two completely different experiences, but at least through this book I was able to share a piece of our hearts, our lives, and perhaps a glimpse inside of missionary life.

I wanted the very last words of this book to be something you could hold onto, something you could use. I thought about profound scriptures and deep things. But alas, this is the best advice I can offer: TRUST IN GOD above all else.

Trust Him to lead and guide you. Use this book in accordance with the measure of faith which was given to you (Romans 12:3), and press in. Press on. Seek God fully and desperately if you feel led into foreign missions. Be true to what God speaks to you. Seek, hear and obey. A life fulfilled by being in step with God's timing is *priceless* and will give you *full satisfaction* in life, knowing you are where you should be . . . all because you followed His voice.

God bless you!

James M. Xavier

The writing of this handbook would not have been possible without the help and loving influence of Pastor Nils and Andrea Olson who have served as resident missionaries in Japan for almost four decades. They are also our mentors of all things Japanese and have taught us much about the culture and religious climate in Japan.

[1] CIA Factbook 2008

[2] OMF International: http://omf.org

[3] A History of Christianity in Japan: Roman Catholic. Greek Orthodox, and Protestant Missions by Otis Cary (1982)

[4] About: http://japanesefood.about.com

[5] Smith, William, Dr. "Entry for 'Laying on of hands'." "Smith's Bible Dictionary" 1901.

[6] Bibliography. E. Lohse, TDNT, 9:428-29, 431-34; M. H. Shepherd, IDB, 2:521-22; M. Warkentin, Ordination: A Biblical-Historical View.

[7] Japan-guide.com: http://www.japan-guide.com/e/e2022.html

[8] Japan-guide.com: ttp://www.japan-guide.com/e/e2200.html

Contact Information

The Xavier Family: Jim, Tracy, Sophia, Serena
Missions web site: http://munakatacity.com
Church web site: http://riveroflifefellowship.org
Email: jamesx@munakatabethel.com

For general inquiries or donations, please write to:

In the USA:
River of Life Fellowship
Attn: JAPAN MISSIONS
10626 SE 216th Street
Kent, WA 98031

In JAPAN:
Munakata Bethel Christian Center
2-26-24 Sue
Munakata City, Fukuoka Prefecture
JAPAN 811-3405

Please prayerfully consider donating or pledging financially to Japan missions and the Xavier family as we minister in Japan. With focus on building community, strengthening the local church and future church plants, there is much we can do together!

May God richly bless your missions endeavors.

SPECIAL EDITION
OVER 100 SCRIPTURES ON FAITH AND TRUSTING GOD

Romans 8:28 - And we know that all things work together for good to them that love God, to them who are the called according to [his] purpose.

Proverbs 3:5 - Trust in the LORD with all thine heart; and lean not unto thine own understanding.

Hebrews 13:8 - Jesus Christ the same yesterday, and to day, and for ever.

Deuteronomy 28:1-68 - And it shall come to pass, if thou shalt hearken diligently unto the voice of the LORD thy God, to observe [and] to do all his commandments which I command thee this day, that the LORD thy God will set thee on high above all nations of the earth . . .

Psalms 46:10 - Be still, and know that I [am] God: I will be exalted among the heathen, I will be exalted in the earth.

Romans 15:13 - Now the God of hope fill you with all joy and peace in believing, that ye may abound in hope, through the power of the Holy Ghost.

Proverbs 3:6 - In all thy ways acknowledge him, and he shall direct thy paths.

Mark 5:36 - As soon as Jesus heard the word that was spoken, he saith unto the ruler of the synagogue, Be not afraid, only believe.

Luke 10:27 - And he answering said, Thou shalt love the Lord thy God with all thy heart, and with all thy soul, and with all thy strength, and with all thy mind; and thy neighbour as thyself.

Psalms 46:1 - (To the chief Musician for the sons of Korah, A Song upon Alamoth.) God [is] our refuge and strength, a very present help in trouble.

2 Timothy 3:16-17 - All scripture [is] given by inspiration of God, and [is] profitable for doctrine, for reproof, for correction, for instruction in righteousness . . .

John 14:26 - But the Comforter, [which is] the Holy Ghost, whom the Father will send in my name, he shall teach you all things, and bring all things to your remembrance, whatsoever I have said unto you.

John 14:15 - If ye love me, keep my commandments.

Proverbs 3:1-35 - My son, forget not my law; but let thine heart keep my commandments: (Read More...)

Psalms 127:1 - (A Song of degrees for Solomon.) Except the LORD build the house, they labour in vain that build it: except the LORD keep the city, the watchman waketh [but] in vain.

Psalms 37:4-6 - Delight thyself also in the LORD; and he shall give thee the desires of thine heart . . .

Deuteronomy 28:47-48 - Because thou servedst not the LORD thy God with joyfulness, and with gladness of heart, for the abundance of all [things];   . . .

Matthew 6:25 - Therefore I say unto you, Take no thought for your life, what ye shall eat, or what ye shall drink; nor yet for your body, what ye shall put on. Is not the life more than meat, and the body than raiment?

Philippians 2:3 - [Let] nothing [be done] through strife or vainglory; but in lowliness of mind let each esteem other better than themselves.

1 Samuel 13:22-23 - So it came to pass in the day of battle, that there was neither sword nor spear found in the hand of any of the people that [were] with Saul and Jonathan: but with Saul and with Jonathan his son was there found . . .

Ephesians 2:8 - For by grace are ye saved through faith; and that not of yourselves: [it is] the gift of God:

2 Corinthians 5:7 - (For we walk by faith, not by sight:)

Hebrews 11:6 - But without faith [it is] impossible to please [him]: for he that cometh to God must believe that he is, and [that] he is a rewarder of them that diligently seek him.

1 John 5:4 - For whatsoever is born of God overcometh the world: and this is the victory that overcometh the world, [even] our faith.

Mark 9:23 - Jesus said unto him, If thou canst believe, all things [are] possible to him that believeth.

SPECIAL EDITION
OVER 100 SCRIPTURES ON FAITH AND TRUSTING GOD

Luke 17:6 - And the Lord said, If ye had faith as a grain of mustard seed, ye might say unto this sycamine tree, Be thou plucked up by the root, and be thou planted in the sea; and it should obey you.

Matthew 9:22 - But Jesus turned him about, and when he saw her, he said, Daughter, be of good comfort; thy faith hath made thee whole. And the woman was made whole from that hour.

1 John 5:14 - And this is the confidence that we have in him, that, if we ask any thing according to his will, he heareth us:

Philippians 4:13 - I can do all things through Christ which strengtheneth me.

Ephesians 2:8-9 - For by grace are ye saved through faith; and that not of yourselves: [it is] the gift of God: . . .

Hebrews 11:1 - Now faith is the substance of things hoped for, the evidence of things not seen.

Psalms 40:4 - Blessed [is] that man that maketh the LORD his trust, and respecteth not the proud, nor such as turn aside to lies.

James 1:3 - Knowing [this], that the trying of your faith worketh patience.

Luke 7:50 - And he said to the woman, Thy faith hath saved thee; go in peace.

Mark 11:23 - For verily I say unto you, That whosoever shall say unto this mountain, Be thou removed, and be thou cast into the sea; and shall not doubt in his heart, but shall believe that those things which he saith shall come to pass; he shall have whatsoever he saith.

Matthew 9:29 - Then touched he their eyes, saying, According to your faith be it unto you.

Mark 9:24 - And straightway the father of the child cried out, and said with tears, Lord, I believe; help thou mine unbelief.

James 2:24 - Ye see then how that by works a man is justified, and not by faith only.

Hebrews 13:5 - [Let your] conversation [be] without covetousness; [and be] content with such things as ye have: for he hath said, I will never leave thee, nor forsake thee.

John 3:36 - He that believeth on the Son hath everlasting life: and he that believeth not the Son shall not see life; but the wrath of God abideth on him.

1 Timothy 4:10 - For therefore we both labour and suffer reproach, because we trust in the living God, who is the Saviour of all men, specially of those that believe.

Mark 11:22-24 - And Jesus answering saith unto them, Have faith in God. . . .

Acts 26:18 - To open their eyes, [and] to turn [them] from darkness to light, and [from] the power of Satan unto God, that they may receive forgiveness of sins, and inheritance among them which are sanctified by faith that is in me.

Mark 5:25-34 - And a certain woman, which had an issue of blood twelve years . . .

Hebrews 13:6 - So that we may boldly say, The Lord [is] my helper, and I will not fear what man shall do unto me.

2 Timothy 1:12 - For the which cause I also suffer these things: nevertheless I am not ashamed: for I know whom I have believed, and am persuaded that he is able to keep that which I have committed unto him against that day.

Acts 3:16 - And his name through faith in his name hath made this man strong, whom ye see and know: yea, the faith which is by him hath given him this perfect soundness in the presence of you all.

James 1:12 - Blessed [is] the man that endureth temptation: for when he is tried, he shall receive the crown of life, which the Lord hath promised to them that love him.

1 Peter 1:7 - That the trial of your faith, being much more precious than of gold that perisheth, though it be tried with fire, might be found unto praise and honour and glory at the appearing of Jesus Christ:

Ephesians 6:16 - Above all, taking the shield of faith, wherewith ye shall be able to quench all the fiery darts of the wicked.

SPECIAL EDITION
OVER 100 SCRIPTURES ON FAITH AND TRUSTING GOD

Galatians 5:22 - But the fruit of the Spirit is love, joy, peace, longsuffering, gentleness, goodness, faith,

Romans 8:28 - And we know that all things work together for good to them that love God, to them who are the called according to [his] purpose.

Matthew 8:2 - And, behold, there came a leper and worshipped him, saying, Lord, if thou wilt, thou canst make me clean.

1 Corinthians 2:5 - That your faith should not stand in the wisdom of men, but in the power of God.

John 6:69 - And we believe and are sure that thou art that Christ, the Son of the living God.

John 3:16 - For God so loved the world, that he gave his only begotten Son, that whosoever believeth in him should not perish, but have everlasting life.

Psalms 18:6 - In my distress I called upon the LORD, and cried unto my God: he heard my voice out of his temple, and my cry came before him, [even] into his ears.

Romans 15:13 - Now the God of hope fill you with all joy and peace in believing, that ye may abound in hope, through the power of the Holy Ghost.

Luke 5:5 - And Simon answering said unto him, Master, we have toiled all the night, and have taken nothing: nevertheless at thy word I will let down the net.

Matthew 9:21 - For she said within herself, If I may but touch his garment, I shall be whole.

Isaiah 40:31 - But they that wait upon the LORD shall renew [their] strength; they shall mount up with wings as eagles; they shall run, and not be weary; [and] they shall walk, and not faint.

Matthew 9:18 - While he spake these things unto them, behold, there came a certain ruler, and worshipped him, saying, My daughter is even now dead: but come and lay thy hand upon her, and she shall live.

1 Samuel 14:6 - And Jonathan said to the young man that bare his armour, Come, and let us go over unto the garrison of these uncircumcised: it may be that the LORD will work for us: for [there is] no restraint to the LORD to save by many or by few.

Romans 3:22-28 - Even the righteousness of God [which is] by faith of Jesus Christ unto all and upon all them that believe: for there is no difference: . . .

John 6:68 - Then Simon Peter answered him, Lord, to whom shall we go? thou hast the words of eternal life.

Habakkuk 2:4 - Behold, his soul [which] is lifted up is not upright in him: but the just shall live by his faith.

Isaiah 55:11 - So shall my word be that goeth forth out of my mouth: it shall not return unto me void, but it shall accomplish that which I please, and it shall prosper [in the thing] whereto I sent it.

Hebrews 11:4 - By faith Abel offered unto God a more excellent sacrifice than Cain, by which he obtained witness that he was righteous, God testifying of his gifts: and by it he being dead yet speaketh.

Ephesians 6:10-18 - Finally, my brethren, be strong in the Lord, and in the power of his might. . . .

John 20:31 - But these are written, that ye might believe that Jesus is the Christ, the Son of God; and that believing ye might have life through his name.

Matthew 17:20 - And Jesus said unto them, Because of your unbelief: for verily I say unto you, If ye have faith as a grain of mustard seed, ye shall say unto this mountain, Remove hence to yonder place; and it shall remove; and nothing shall be impossible unto you.

Hebrews 6:13-15 - For when God made promise to Abraham, because he could swear by no greater, he sware by himself, . . .

Colossians 2:7 - Rooted and built up in him, and stablished in the faith, as ye have been taught, abounding therein with thanksgiving.

SPECIAL EDITION
OVER 100 SCRIPTURES ON FAITH AND TRUSTING GOD

Philippians 1:27 - Only let your conversation be as it becometh the gospel of Christ: that whether I come and see you, or else be absent, I may hear of your affairs, that ye stand fast in one spirit, with one mind striving together for the faith of the gospel;

1 Samuel 17:37 - David said moreover, The LORD that delivered me out of the paw of the lion, and out of the paw of the bear, he will deliver me out of the hand of this Philistine. And Saul said unto David, Go, and the LORD be with thee.

Revelation 3:20 - Behold, I stand at the door, and knock: if any man hear my voice, and open the door, I will come in to him, and will sup with him, and he with me.

Revelation 2:19 - I know thy works, and charity, and service, and faith, and thy patience, and thy works; and the last [to be] more than the first.

Hebrews 11:24-28 - By faith Moses, when he was come to years, refused to be called the son of Pharaoh's . . .

Hebrews 10:39 - But we are not of them who draw back unto perdition; but of them that believe to the saving of the soul.

Hebrews 10:35 - Cast not away therefore your confidence, which hath great recompence of reward.

Galatians 2:16 - Knowing that a man is not justified by the works of the law, but by the faith of Jesus Christ, even we have believed in Jesus Christ, that we might be justified by the faith of Christ, and not by the works of the law: for by the works of the law shall no flesh be justified.

Romans 8:39 - Nor height, nor depth, nor any other creature, shall be able to separate us from the love of God, which is in Christ Jesus our Lord.

Romans 8:37 - Nay, in all these things we are more than conquerors through him that loved us.

Romans 8:35 - Who shall separate us from the love of Christ? [shall] tribulation, or distress, or persecution, or famine, or nakedness, or peril, or sword?

Psalms 7:1 - (Shiggaion of David, which he sang unto the LORD, concerning the words of Cush the Benjamite.) O LORD my God, in thee do I put my trust: save me from all them that persecute me, and deliver me:

2 Kings 18:5 - He trusted in the LORD God of Israel; so that after him was none like him among all the kings of Judah, nor [any] that were before him.

2 Peter 3:13 - Nevertheless we, according to his promise, look for new heavens and a new earth, wherein dwelleth righteousness.

James 1:6 - But let him ask in faith, nothing wavering. For he that wavereth is like a wave of the sea driven with the wind and tossed.

Hebrews 13:7 - Remember them which have the rule over you, who have spoken unto you the word of God: whose faith follow, considering the end of [their] conversation.

Hebrews 11:7 - By faith Noah, being warned of God of things not seen as yet, moved with fear, prepared an ark to the saving of his house; by the which he condemned the world, and became heir of the righteousness which is by faith.

Hebrews 10:38 - Now the just shall live by faith: but if [any man] draw back, my soul shall have no pleasure in him.

Hebrews 6:12 - That ye be not slothful, but followers of them who through faith and patience inherit the promises.

2 Timothy 4:7 - I have fought a good fight, I have finished [my] course, I have kept the faith:

1 Timothy 1:19 - Holding faith, and a good conscience; which some having put away concerning faith have made shipwreck:

Romans 10:6-10 - But the righteousness which is of faith speaketh on this wise, Say not in thine heart, Who shall ascend into heaven? (that is, to bring Christ down [from above]:) . . .

SPECIAL EDITION
OVER 100 SCRIPTURES ON FAITH AND TRUSTING GOD

Mark 16:16 - He that believeth and is baptized shall be saved; but he that believeth not shall be damned.

Matthew 13:58 - And he did not many mighty works there because of their unbelief.

Matthew 9:28 - And when he was come into the house, the blind men came to him: and Jesus saith unto them, Believe ye that I am able to do this? They said unto him, Yea, Lord.

Hebrews 12:2 - Looking unto Jesus the author and finisher of [our] faith; who for the joy that was set before him endured the cross, despising the shame, and is set down at the right hand of the throne of God.

2 Timothy 2:11-13 - [It is] a faithful saying: For if we be dead with [him], we shall also live with [him]: . . .

2 Timothy 1:13 - Hold fast the form of sound words, which thou hast heard of me, in faith and love which is in Christ Jesus.

1 Timothy 3:9 - Holding the mystery of the faith in a pure conscience.

Colossians 1:23 - If ye continue in the faith grounded and settled, and [be] not moved away from the hope of the gospel, which ye have heard, [and] which was preached to every creature which is under heaven; whereof I Paul am made a minister;

Galatians 5:6 - For in Jesus Christ neither circumcision availeth any thing, nor uncircumcision; but faith which worketh by love.

2 Corinthians 4:16-18 - For which cause we faint not; but though our outward man perish, yet the inward [man] is renewed day by day. . . .

Romans 10:17 - So then faith [cometh] by hearing, and hearing by the word of God.

Romans 3:23 - For all have sinned, and come short of the glory of God;

Jude 1:21 - Keep yourselves in the love of God, looking for the mercy of our Lord Jesus Christ unto eternal life.

1 Peter 1:21 - Who by him do believe in God, that raised him up from the dead, and gave him glory; that your faith and hope might be in God.

1 Peter 1:8 - Whom having not seen, ye love; in whom, though now ye see [him] not, yet believing, ye rejoice with joy unspeakable and full of glory: